RILKE AND BENVENUTA

". . . Much has become buried and can hardly be told, but if, one day, the hour you know of should come (and it is certain that I could then do no other than unquestioningly affirm it), then bear testimony, for you are called to be my witness, you who hold the legacy of my life in your blessed hands" (p. 190).

By way of fulfilment of these words of Rilke's, written to the author, this book of thanks is now offered to the public. Rilke's letters to the author, his talks with her and notes from her diaries for the years 1914 to 1928, form the authentic foundation of the book. It contains much that was decisive in Rilke's life, known hitherto only to a few initiates. May these confessions be accepted with the same reverence with which they are offered.

RILKE AND BENVENUTA

By

MAGDA VON HATTINGBERG

✻

A BOOK OF THANKS

✻

Translated from the German
by CYRUS BROOKS

W. W. NORTON & COMPANY, INC.

PUBLISHERS   NEW YORK

This work originally appeared
in German under the title
Rilke und Benvenuta

Contents

Am 18. (Vormittag)

Deine zwei Brief und die Carte vom 16. —
Jetzt aufsteht eine gewisse neue Sehnsucht, nicht
etwa zwischen diesem Bogen und dem Abtritt;
blatt, nein, eine ganz aufgelassene, an die sicher
noch nie jemand gedacht hat. Stell dir vor:
zwischen dem in der Lade aufgeschlagenen, lang,
sam zunehmenden Tage, Brief für Dich und die,
für nebenseits, durch die ich recht zu Dir hinein,
trete, nur um dir zu sagen: Lieb, lieber,
liebe —

Hier denn zu einer das zu sagen versuchen,
wie sehr das Wunderbare in der Welt ist, nicht
nur da und dort nicht nur an irgend einem
Ziel, nicht nur gegen nahen Händen über —,
nein da in uns, in jeder Halle unseres Wesens;
und wenn seine Allgegenwärtigkeit uns plötzlich
sicher wird, — siehe, dann schlägt es uns aus dem
unbegreiflich Außerordentlichen das es ist, ins
das heilig Natürliche — ins Gesetz, ohne das
wir gar nicht wären.

Rainer Maria Rilke's handwriting.

Beginnings

ALONG the twilit streets bright candles, gingerbreads and silvery stars glistened on the decorated Christmas trees in the shop-windows. I walked through the town, looking at the treasures thus displayed—dolls and other toys, fine silver, leather bags, silks and costly etchings. I wanted to buy myself a book. No specific book, but one that would give me something quite different from all I had ever learned or read before. Somewhere in the world there must, I felt, be a consoling voice, one that could resolve all that was sad and frightening in a period of inner disappointment from which I had scarcely emerged, a voice that could give meaning to my broken youth and a fresh glimpse of life.

I went into a little bookshop, where I knew the proprietor. "It must be different from all other books," I said. "A wonderful book."

The old man nodded as though he understood. He made no answer, but went to one of the large, dark, polished cases, took out a slim, greenish-black volume, and laid it in front of me. "This is it," he said.

I opened it at the title-page. Rainer Maria Rilke, I read, *Tales of the Almighty*[1]—and asked, "Who is Rainer Maria Rilke?"

My old friend took the book, wrapped it in paper, handed it to me and said solemnly, "A poet, a real, unique poet. Everything else is in the book."

So, through the snow-bright Christmas streets, I carried home the *Tales of the Almighty*, and it was as though my steps had grown lighter, as though, consoled by an approaching and half-expected miracle, I held in my hands the light of a star.

[1] *Geschichten vom lieben Gott.* The title of the published English translation—*Stories of God*—fails to suggest the playful quality of the title in the original German.

I

All that night I read—or rather worshipped—in Rainer Maria Rilke's book, though until a few hours before I had never even heard his name. I read the story of Michelangelo and of old Timofei; I read of the cripple Ewald, and of the man who received a letter, of children, and of death—death that could not kill love, and had to bloom, a dark flower, in the garden of lovers. It was as though the pain I had recently suffered lay far behind me, dry and shrunken in the past. Only once before, when still half a child, had I drawn comfort, in an hour of inner need and helplessness, from a book. Then the words were from *Morgenröte*—"I found it, my brothers, I found the spring where the rabble does not drink". But Nietzsche's austerity, almost painful, like a too brilliant light, was too high and far for me to reach. Here in the *Tales of the Almighty* a man was speaking who, so it seemed to me, knew everything; more, a man who perceived the inexpressible in, behind and above phenomena, and succeeded for the first time in giving it words; who comprehended all things, love and horror; for whom pain and joy, the darkest blackness and the brightest light, were brothers. It was as if all the comfort, happiness and understanding in the world were streaming into my receptive heart. I knew that with such a revelation I ought to begin a new life, obeying Leonardo's immortal words: "He cannot turn back who is tied to a star".

One evening, a few days later, I was sitting alone in my room. The others were happily engaged in the adjoining room with tea and cakes and talk of everyday affairs. They were in a quiet, cheerful holiday mood, but I was mentally far away, as though in the solitude of some spacious countryside. I took a sheet of paper and began to write. It was my first letter to Rainer Maria Rilke. I did not reflect, indeed I hardly knew I was writing; it was no more than a strong inward urge to thank him, simply to thank him.

I wrote: "Dear Friend, Your *Tales of the Almighty* are dedicated to Ellen Key. In the charming dedication you say that no one has liked them better than she, and that therefore they belong to her. I have never yet wished to be anyone but myself, but now nothing would please me more than to be metamorphosed into Ellen Key, so that that dedication would be mine; I am convinced that my love for the *Tales of the Almighty* is greater than anyone else's in the world."

I told him that his book had brought me great comfort, and, since it was so full of music, I wished I could express in music all my joy and thankfulness to him, for music was my natural element and exceeded the power of words.

So far was I from any thought of an answer that I wrote only my name and not my address on the back of the envelope. I did not know where he lived, so I sent the letter to his publisher. And thus the words of a stranger to a poet went forth into the world.

A week later, one clear, sunny winter morning, an express letter arrived from Paris. The handwriting was unfamiliar; it was beautiful, gentle but firm, light and joyous. The envelope was sealed with a dark green, oval seal; there was no name under it. I did not know why, but at sight of that writing, my heart beat fast and I suddenly thought with a sense of jubilation, All the flags are flying!

It was some time before I dared open it. Inside were many closely-written pages, and, on the last, his name. I was reading— though still I could hardly believe it—Rilke's reply; I was holding Rilke's letter in my hand.

"Paris, 26 January, 1914.

"GOOD FRIEND,

"Let me take in that rich tone, for with your letter it is becoming part of me. What joy that you wrote it, and how good that there were obstacles to metamorphosing yourself into Ellen Key! It would have complicated the situation exceedingly. All the more so because, since the *Tales of the Almighty* were written, we have each been thoroughly dissatisfied with the other's production. . . . But perhaps all I have done since then is, for you too, false or insignificant; if so, I must pass back what is good in your letter to the address, now most uncertain, of that young man who told his tales about the Almighty so many, remarkable years ago . . .

"To be frank, does he deserve it? I rather grudge it him; it seems to me that he limned the contours of his temperament too light-heartedly; you do him much more honour than is justified. Oh, I cannot really tell you anything about him; perhaps, after all, you give him his due; but however much you may pamper him, I still have this advantage: he will never hear your music, while *I shall*, or so I hope."

And I read on as in a dream:

". . . when you were abroad, why didn't you come suddenly through Southern Spain? How I would have welcomed you! My heart would have built you arch upon arch of triumph. You would have seen your music making one continuous entry, for your arrival would have taken place in the depths of me, where I myself have never been."

A stranger, far away, was writing to me as a familiar friend. I could hardly believe it. I read on:

" . . . just think, I passed that winter in a little Spanish town not far from Gibraltar. I had been for some time in Toledo . . . I can assure you, it was unique, as if one imagined it to oneself, and yet, every day and every one of those incredible nights, there it was. As an apparition exceeds the actual stature of a man, so did that town, that landscape, exceed actual landscape as we know it. . . . In Ronda (that was the town in the South of Spain) it suddenly became clear to me that my sense of sight is too overburdened: there too the sky staged the same pomps and the cloud-shadows brought the same expression to the earth's substance—there I sat as though at the end of vision, as though I must now go blind with the impressions I had absorbed, or, if destiny and being are inexhaustible, perceive the world thenceforth through some other, quite different sense. Music, music—that would have been it.

"Once someone was playing an instrument in my little hotel. I could not see him; I sat in the next room and in that wondrous element (I scarcely know it, and it has always been too strong for me) I felt the world relax and loosen; it gave me an effortless, almost overpowering, happiness to feel the world enter into me from thence, for my hearing is new like the sole of a baby's foot . . ."

A poet wrote those words, who had experienced the purest music. To me they were like a song that I had never heard and yet had known from the beginning. I felt as though he were actually speaking to me.

". . . now I live here again entirely without music and in much inward stress. . . . But your music lies before me like some season yet to be; unless later it turns against me, it may happen somewhere, sometime, that I go out to meet it, as one goes to Sicily to meet the Spring, which in the North keeps one waiting and doubting."

Never had anyone spoken to me like this, but it was not a dream. I really held those wondrous pages in my hands—and what they brought was no isolated greeting, for he wrote: "Do not let the new, precious fire go out," and ". . . I am grateful and devoted to you.

"RAINER MARIA RILKE"

Yes, it was a comforting voice that spoke to me in all the many letters that now began to reach me daily. It was the voice of the life-spirit raised above all human things, yet deeply aware of them, the spirit to which God spoke intimately, which knew the limits of suffering. It was as though a mind spoke to me, hidden in the earthly life of humanity, enduring human life and yet understanding and affirming it illimitably:

". . . it is Sunday; I will keep it holy and write to you, for now you hold in your hands a wonderful future for me, a future that has the power to bring upon me storms, tempests and clear weather, nothing less than the convulsions of the universe, just as it will. My friend, I do not ask when that will be, but it will be. I never asked, not even when, as a helpless child, I was sent to the military academy. Life could never enter there, not even a single breath of my own life. And yet everything was there; yes, there was always too much; all the stresses of life come from its richness."

He was always full of a longing for music:

"I was almost afraid of music, except when it was performed in a cathedral and went straight up to God, without tarrying with me on the way. In Egypt I was told—and I understood it—that in the Old Kingdom (it is assumed) music was forbidden. It could only be performed before the God, produced for his sake, as though he alone could bear the excess and seduction of its sweetness and to all lesser folk it would be fatal. Is not that true, my friend? . . . Or is music the resurrection of the dead? Does one die on the verge of it and arise radiantly in it, no longer a destroyer? But has my heart the strength to die in it completely in order to emerge complete? . . . I remember I used to think on great steppes that I had become a hero, simply because the clouds on spring evenings were piled in such audacious shapes on the horizon. But then it was also possible for a man to wreck his life because somewhere he had heard in passing the note of a violin, which deflected his whole will into a denser fate. When I remember what primitive force resided in some stray scrap of old music of the kind I have sometimes heard in Italy or Spain or South Russia, it seems to me that Beethoven was a lord of the hosts, holding sway over the powers, tearing dangers asunder to throw across them a bridge of radiant salvation . . ."

In these letters Rilke poured out before me almost inexhaustible riches and showed me a trust as deep as it was difficult to comprehend.

". . . dear heart, how my heart streams, yes streams, towards you—all the letters that would take years to write, I should like to write them all at once. There are such mornings by the sea, gay and strong; all the waves try to run in together. . . . There is pure joy between us, and how clear it is; we can see the most distant places and the bells swing almost visibly through the receptive air. . . . Friend, blessed, joyous one, untamable spirit, chance has sent my books one by one to your heart, books I wrote long ago. Who was I then? Who am I now? How would it all have turned out if you had read a prose work in two volumes, in which I tried to work up stores of old grief, unaware that I was only just beginning my afflictions. Unspeakable times! Not that I should have lost my faith in greatness and grown timid —I should certainly have gone on. . . . But I feel as though I had walked straight ahead into a mountain and—by persistent miracles against nature—breathed its stone till my own being is stone. Now I don't care for 'miracles'; my preference is all for nature, so I sometimes felt like a monster in my mountain. . . . I hoped that someone would come with a pickaxe and get me out, pick me out and lay me down in a meadow under the wind— someone who would say nothing but would understand, and be *there*. Probably I shouted till a few passers-by actually set to work to dig me out, but when they had done so it was all useless. I have no experience of people and in the end I asked them to go away and, as soon as they had gone, I crawled back into my mountain, for outside I merely gave myself away and got nothing for it, while the stone at least held me together. . . . I had to tell you this: as I write, I am much more like the man in my fairy-tale than the young man of long ago, whose books have pleased and moved you. The present man (who admits no one intimately to himself) would write to all others telling them not to come. To you (his unexpected friend, in whom he is gaining the deepest confidence) he writes: act according to your pleasure; that cannot be other than right, for it has on its side the power and the glory . . ."

In these letters Rilke told the whole story of his life, from that half-happy, half-frightened childhood to which he repeatedly returned:

". . . once we lived everything, for we were immature; I think we fully experienced horror . . . we did not know it was horror; and joy too—we did not know there was such a thing, it was too rich for our hearts—and perhaps the whole of love. Playmates, girls, did I not love you? How I rushed to meet you— and you too were breathless, exhaling your hot fragrance, like fields of clover in high summer. We stood far apart, but the ball brought it me from your hands—a glow half of your body, half of your soul. When you came, or were to come (and that 'were to come' seemed mysteriously laid down in the cosmic order—that 'were to come', at four o'clock, 'or rather a little earlier'), how my room was swept and dusted: there sat my dolls, marvelling, the door-handles shone. . . . And the other girls, already grown-up, whom I had hardly noticed. One day they were quieter than usual; I watched them over the coffee-cups and the quietest was sitting opposite me—how beautiful she was! I realised that her hair was no longer a child's, neatly done by loving hands but the hands of others—now it was *her* hair. . . . Suddenly I asked myself, God knows why, whether she had not just been crying— and then my heart went out to her across the cakes. . . . It was a very one-sided occupation to love a tall, thoughtful girl like that; I laid my cheek against the edge of the table where she had leaned; I saw her coming in the street, recognisable at a distance through all the disguises of her loveliness. . . . The troubadour's noble longing to serve, how it came over me, first pride of chivalry, first melancholy—because she would never know of it: gracious feelings, worn one over the other, like armour over a silken doublet of pale rose. And while those around me grew thin with anxiety in their efforts to protect me from the slightest cold, there was no inch of my body, day or night, that did not yearn to die for her."

Rilke wrote about everything in his childhood, great and small, about his parents' house, the spectral piety of his mother, of whom he was not afraid to say bitterly that she "prayed as others drink coffee". During his early years she was very unhappy because he was a boy; up to the age of six she made him wear girl's clothes and called him "Sophie". When he was still quite small she made him dust the furniture and do girl's work about the house. How many memories he shared with me of the strange, rich, inner life of his childhood:

"Sometimes memories come from far away. Yesterday morning I saw the following: in my little street, a man was standing on a ladder, openly and with the clear conscience of his honest trade, painting the woodwork of a shop to look like marble . . . this went on in all cheerfulness and innocence until a little girl crossed the street, stopped in front of the paintwork, cocked her fresh-combed head to one side like a sparrow and called up to him: '*Ah, que beau, ah, que beau!*' There was such an astonishing irony in her cheeky, bird-like voice that the man on the ladder must have gone quite dizzy. I laughed, but, once round the corner, it came back to me that at about the same age I paid great attention to the difference between real and imitation marble. If we entered a restaurant or the stairway of a block of flats, I waited till I was unobserved and then immediately felt the wall or the nearest pillar; if it failed to pass the test, I was careful not to betray it, and I believe I tacitly paid it a kind of sympathy. . . . For then how far away was such a little boy from irony. Who could have understood me? . . . When I think of my father, I am almost certain that he knew nothing of this ; I believe he was incapable of love; right up to the end he had a kind of speechless anxiety towards me, an attitude to which I was practically defenceless, and which probably cost him more than the mightiest love . . ."

Thus we conversed from a distance, and when I wrote it was always with deep gratitude. But I could not believe him when he said that I, to whom he gave so richly, gave him courage and happiness in return. I did not dare believe it, and yet the incredible must have been true, for he wrote:

"Dear one, nearest, sister, are you[1] there? Is it possible?— Did God send you to me in the years of my mortal need to give me strength to survive? Can I sense the world, breathe its air, in the certitude that it contains you, my friend, as I know it

---

[1] *Du.* Hitherto Rilke has addressed her with the formal *Sie.*

contains God?—God, whom I have felt so illimitably in the joy of my work, as you have in your music. . . . The suddenly felt '*Du*' must not replace the earlier word; I want to call you (*Dir*) everything, to use every name, and thus make plain to myself that you (*Sie*) are nearness and distance, that you (*Du*) are frankness and my refuge from it . . .''

And so I received afresh in each new letter the infinite bounty of a candid heart and guarded it reverently. He told me of his frightened years in the military academy, of his first love and first disappointment, of his marriage and its dissolution, of his child, of the sublimity of his great friendship with Rodin, of the pain of misunderstanding, of travel, work and loneliness—and of the dæmons in his nature:

". . . if I tell you, Benvenuta, of this sickness that pierces deep into the soul and spreads along the whole body, this sense of being distorted like something bent to uses for which it was never intended—Benvenuta, you would not believe the hateful feelings that go through my soul at the sight of human conditions. Save me from that too. How often I assure you that I will not yield to the shadow of a thought that I could not confess to you; that assurance excludes none, not the cruellest, not the basest; only that some hint or provocation should tempt me—that is excluded.''

Moving and sacred was his trust when he spoke to me of the ultimate things of his own life, and I understood, or rather, I painfully divined, that, despite all his yearning for another person, he had to be and remain alone. It was his fate and his tragedy "not to be able to bind the heart's powers to human beings", however fervently he longed to do so. He, the most understanding, the most consoling of men, suffered from a nameless affliction that lay exclusively in himself and in his mortal substance. Sometimes I thought these ideas were foolish, for letters came which radiated all the sunshine and brightness of a spring day; at such times there was something winged and exultant in his writing:

"My dear heart, what purity, what brightness, what storms in my soul on your account! It is because my thoughts acquire purity in you, and no impure thought can exist since it cannot exist in you. The life of the mind for which I have been struggling all these unbearable years (do you understand, the mind that is so mightily mind that it can sweep all things into itself, excluding nothing), that infinite life of the mind comes true for me in you; I glimpse, as it were, a country of all innocence. . . . I feel it—it is your nature to grasp me as a whole, you greater circle round the infinite circle of my heart . . ."

My friend revealed everything in these indescribably wonderful letters—and how well he could describe, with his own warm, gentle humour, himself and other people and things:

". . . just think, I have had a visitor (if I open the door I'm lost) —a painter, seeking information about a new publishing house, a new periodical (good God, how many of them there are! And how bad!) In short, we agreed that contemporary art is following curious paths, and that we had been taught otherwise. He grew quite old as we discussed it: our apprentice days dropped away, submerged in the immemorial beneath the surge of the new. Not I, I didn't get old, I'm still an apprentice. When he had got so old that he could only just walk, I quickly presented him with a book . . ."

I came to know the little world around him: the old newspaper-woman at the corner, the restaurant where he took his meals, the *femme de ménage* with her "ever fresh supply of small-talk". He wrote so vividly of it all that I felt I saw these people and things physically before my eyes.

". . . let me tell you about my post-office. It is the nearest I can get to you; then I have to leave to other people the letters I hand over here so rich and solitary. You have no idea how such post-offices in France are—how shall I put it?—constituted, with their warmed-up pens and blotting-paper, for nothing is lost in their economy. Behind the barred windows at the counter are women and little *pneumatique* boys with dreamy, absent eyes and open mouths—into which one is tempted to slip a rolled-up card. . . . But I'm particularly set on another character. . . . Dogs are not admitted, so if you have a dog, you leave it without, and there it sits with its head on one side, wondering why its master keeps on sending out the wrong people, instead of coming himself in his own unsurpassed reality—well, then it may happen that this 'character' informs the dog through a chink in the door (the sacred door of hope) that all is not lost, that he is taking care of its master somewhere inside. When you see the 'character' back in his place, he turns out to be a very little old man at a very little old desk. I assume that his vitality was not exhausted before he entered his present employment, which is the following: every morning he cleans up, so to speak, by a method of his own invention: he searches for three or four pieces of rag, which he has left in various places, finds them, looks at them sternly through his spectacles and leaves them in slightly different places. . . . Later on he was sleeping at his desk, although the room was full of commotion, and in the background the postmaster was conversing rather loudly with a gentleman. The gentleman left, others left, I left, and as I did so I gathered from the shouts behind me that the postmaster wanted his gentleman back again. In such cases one called for—you can imagine whom. Well, my dear, I turned round and there was the old man in a state of unspeakable distress, trying to find a gentleman he had never seen. For a few seconds he was, from his standpoint, optically right in thinking that all the men whose backs he could see had come out of the post-office, issuing endlessly from the reality of the post-office as effects issue from a cause. The old man stood dumbfounded before this abstraction; involuntarily he retired into himself, into his own being, where a moment before he had enjoyed all the security of sleep, and in that state he was bound to meet me—we were both charmed. . . . So I bethought myself and hastily chose for him the most probable among the departing backs. Oh, Benvenuta, what is all this I have been telling you? . . ."

Lightly and affectionately as he saw the world in its brighter aspects, it could be terrifying when the tragic element in his own soul arose and threatened to overwhelm him:

". . . what ghosts everywhere, Benvenuta. . . . Once I had been out in the country all day and came back late in the evening: on the landing outside the door of my flat was a great mass of flowers, country flowers, not tied in bunches, and tall sprays of peach and apple blossom, the finest that one could find. . . . Tired to death I laboured for two hours to dispose of them. No pot seemed tall enough for the heavy, sprawling shoots and when I thought I had finished, there were still more—I found them by the light of my candle on the floor, in arm-chairs, lying across my books. I searched for another pot; the candle dazzled me in the lofty darkness; I could not find the flowers again but I found others. How exhausted they looked, as though in a swoon! I

B

knelt down and put the candle on the floor and tried to sort them out. When I looked up, there was the shadow of those sprays on the wall, hostile, like a gigantic claw. When at last it was done I knocked over in passing the tall pot with the sprays of blossom and a flood of water poured towards me—Benvenuta, is there a hell?—those night hours were like a bitter grief, pressed into my heart in splinters, and I had to dissolve them bit by bit, and had nothing to do it with but my own warmth. Oh, forgive me for writing you all this—dear one!"

Such letters often filled me with oppressive fears for his health, even for his life. When in my anxiety I wrote that perhaps he should consult a doctor, he refused to hear of it; he even comforted me:

". . . I have no fear of the morbid, for I will not cling to it, merely pass through and survive it. I believe that as long as one does not misunderstand it and give it free play, there is nothing more transient than morbidity; being unreal, it tries to escape as soon as confronted with something positive. . . . I have never been able to establish contact with a doctor. They start with distrusting what one says, and immediately I have a feeling that I am facing a stranger. What does the fellow want between my nature and me? We exchange a glance behind his back, my nature and I, such a friendly, intimate glance, Benvenuta, as though we were suddenly in complete accord."

Such words gave me new hope and I wrote full of happiness and confidence. He accepted these letters with all the tenderness of his nature:

". . . Oh, near one, nearest, innermost, if only I hadn't to be always doing things, seeing people, reading letters from strangers and even going out to my silly little restaurant; if only God would be sympathetic and feed me discreetly at home by means of a raven, and I could simply sit here always, like 'Hieronymus in his box' and write you letters. Then if the raven comes with his nice round cosmic rolls, I nod in the manner such birds understand and say, 'Thank you. Put them over there, please'—and forget all about it. Forget it, my love, and go on living a thousandfold in my faith in you. This is how I feel: You are there—that ought to be breath and food and drink to me. . . . For we have one thing—our joy—which God brought forth in the beginning at the creation. No one has ever dared to make use of it, because it looked so unpromising, and so it has come to us fresh from paradise . . ."

An incredible gift had been given me: his joy, his anxieties, his days of trial and his words, "You save me too".

All this brought me the deepest happiness and yet weighed me down with a burden of responsibility almost certainly too heavy to bear. I often asked myself, "Can one, dare one, influence the inmost nature of another person? Is it possible to save a person from the tragic elements inherent in himself? Must not a man shape his own inner destiny for himself, quite alone?" How could I presume to exercise a decisive influence over him? Of course such thoughts struggled with the phantom of a great hope —that it might still be miraculously possible to vanquish those sinister elements by inconquerable faith. Then came a letter in which Rilke wrote again of his precarious mental and physical health. He had been advised to submit to the treatment of the psycho-analyst, Professor Freud, but rejected the idea with great vehemence. I understood him only too well. I had met Professor Freud only twice, but his personality, his way of speaking, above all his theories had impressed me unfavourably; indeed I felt disgusted by them. Rilke wrote about psycho-analysis and the advice of those friends who wished to convert him to Freud's ideas:

". . . luckily it had already become quite clear to me that nothing could be more disastrous, more fatal even, than to expose myself to the effects of such a treatment, even to the smallest extent. The more I learned of the aims and progress of analysis, the more I was forced to realise that it would produce nothing short of disintegration in a life of which the strongest impulses arose from the fact *that it did not know itself*, that it was inexhaustibly related through its own deep, psychic mystery with all the mysteries of the world, even with God himself, whence it was secretly and generously sustained.

"Dear heart, dear, dear girl, there was a moment when, in defence and exorcism, I cried out against myself, for I realised that (for a moment) I had attempted to go too far in tracking down my own complexities. My sister, I gained a new reverence for my inner being, when I saw that I must not let myself be led into it, that I possess it only when, poor as I now am, I lie across its threshold, as a lover lies in poverty before the unexplored heart of the beloved, to which he has no right except she step incomprehensibly forth of her own free will.

"And I promised myself to suffer far more than I have suffered, and rather to perish in my increasing woe than presume to try to look upon the powers that dispose of me deep, deep within: *for in this also is my strength that I do not check the most secret forces in myself.* Benvenuta, Benvenuta to me from everlasting—do we understand one another? . . ."

How often my distant friend had said in his letters that all human influences were disastrous to him, for his whole life was "fiercely battling loneliness" for the sake of his work. And much as I was delighted when he wrote ever more frequently and urgently, "If only we could see each other, if only you would come", yet at the same time I was frightened by it. It seemed to me incredible that I should see Rilke, that I should really hear him speak, who had won everything back for me—the world, life, joy, strength to act—and yet could complain—how often and how hopelessly!—of his own life. This contradiction, which I could hardly understand, sometimes filled me with deep apprehension, for in all the delight of his words there intruded again, suddenly and unexpectedly, a shadow that threatened to destroy it all:

"Benvenuta, most sisterly one, how often there comes into my clear flow towards you the fear—always close and deep—of my own inadequacy; for I know I am not like the days of the year that flow one from the other, but all excess of expression can suddenly turn to its most frigid opposite, like a river that flows with its waters abruptly underground—oh love, when that fear overtakes me, I want to come over to you immediately in my incalculable breadth, but I cannot; I have to break up the fronts of my armies and send them forward man by man through the pass of these inhospitable pages. So must it be when a man yearns for eternal bliss; he feels that with his prayers he comes by it only piecemeal. Ah, he must die if he is to break grandly into it at one burst and make heaven almost quake with the turbulence of his soul. Thus you would feel me and not even be startled, for it would be your nature to grasp me whole. You, genuine child and my sister, dear, dear girl, if only I could swing always between the shadow your hands would make for me and the realm of eternal light that comes from your music! Tell me, shall I still live on the day when all this has been said and fulfilled?

Or shall I die then? It is the testament of my whole life that I make real in you. And who am I, that with a surge of being can write *You*, and seal it with your heart!"

For me his call was like a holy command. I cannot remember the exact words, I only know I wrote him that it would be glorious if we could wait for each other in some strange railway station among totally indifferent people. I mentioned Florence or Lucerne or Geneva. His pleasure streamed back to me:

"Geneva—good heavens, Benvenuta, I have never seen my trunk behave like this; I just looked to see where it was, and it forced its way through the curtain and into my eyes, feeling emptier than ever in its life; it demanded to be packed on the spot, so I have to restrain it, or one fine day it would set off alone for Geneva, empty, with my travelling-rug still on it. Dear heart, is this really possible? . . . Wonderful that it is a town I have never yet visited. First I should like to be with you in places that are quite new to me, as radiantly new as all this, till bit by bit the old places too, as though resurrected, pass retrospectively into our, *our* glory."

In the next few days—news had come meanwhile that I had first to go to Berlin to arrange about a concert—I had a very strange dream which was repeated on three successive nights. I wrote it down and sent it to Rilke in my next letter. It was a dream of Charon and the house of the dead:

I was standing in a grey, square tower, surrounded by dark, still water. There were three big windows in the stone walls; one looked out on the sea, another on the mountains and the third on the life of our time. The third wall had a gateway that led into gloomy depths. Charon was standing in his boat, watching in silence as a procession of men, children, girls and women passed through the gateway into the uncertain regions beyond; once when he turned his head I saw that his eyes were stars.

I had to ring a bell when fresh groups of people moved sadly and with bent heads towards the depths—and the bell repeated with an alarming sound, "When? When?" Through the big window that looked over the sea I suddenly saw innumerable ships approaching the tower. The golden helmets of warriors glinted in the evening light: they had come from a great distance to storm the house of the dead. But when they were quite near, a heavy, grey wall rose up between them and the tower—the shouts and the clink of weapons died away and it was deathly still again.

But a movement arose in front of the window that looked out on the life of our time. There was a street filled with people, vehicles and the traffic of a big town. Through this traffic a child was crossing the road, a doll in its arms, looking down tenderly at the doll—but two great black horses came racing up at a furious speed and dashed the child to the ground. A number of people ran to help it; one lifted it up—it was bleeding from many wounds and held the doll pressed fearfully to its breast, but in its little, dying face the smile still shone like the sun. Charon had turned; he seemed to have forgotten the boat and the crowds of the dead—he stood at the window and looked and looked—and I saw that tears were streaming from his starlike eyes.

Suddenly the bell began to ring of itself; all those who had passed into the depths came back happy and blissful through the dark gateway, and with the full, solemn clangour a choir of singing voices arose: "Look, look, a child has redeemed the world".

The day before I left, Rilke's lovely and welcome answer reached me, and so the circle that began with the *Tales of the Almighty* was closed with these words of his:

"Dear, your dream, do you know what it is? It is the most beautiful of the *Tales of the Almighty*, but it is not to be found in my book, for I did not write it: *You* dreamed it. And there is great, splendid, incomprehensible justice in that."

Anticipation

IN Berlin I stayed at the house of the Delbrücks in Grunewald. For years they had been close friends of mine. Their house was the home of all beautiful things, of the arts and of an understanding humanism. Despite their wealth the rooms were simple and comfortable and gave an impression of peace, happiness, sincerity and deep artistic sensibility. The place of honour in Frau Delbrück's sitting-room was occupied by Rodin's magnificent bronze "The Centaur", while in Delbrück's study was Schadow's marble bust of Frederick the Great. Pictures by famous masters, valuable furniture—family heir-looms—beautiful furnishings of all kinds and a big Bechstein grand piano adorned the house, which stood in a pleasant garden in the Hubertus Allée, then still a very quiet street.

Frau Berta Delbrück was one of those rare women who radiate peace, happiness and a sense of security, and she was very happy when I told her about Rilke. One evening after dinner, when we had listened to music and good talk, we were sitting at the round table in her sitting-room; the children had gone to bed and in this quiet and peaceful atmosphere I read aloud to her from *Malte Laurids Brigge*, a book she had never read.

Before we parted I opened the window and the late winter air blew in from the garden, as we looked up at the stars sparkling above the bare trees. Frau Delbrück said in her gentle voice: "If only Rilke were with us now! Lonely as he is, I think he would feel a bit of home."

Then I knew that I would not go to Geneva, but would ask Rilke to come to me here. I wrote him that it would be good for us to meet in this house of dear people that was so like home to me; I described the place with all the love I felt for it, told him of the forest-paths in Grunewald, of late winter walks one could take, of the still lakes, the garden where snowdrops were blooming.

The bare landscape acquired a mystery and wonder in

anticipation of the presence of my friend. His answer was a reflection of my own happiness, a reflection of my suddenly re-awakened hope that his life could be freed from its burdens, could be saved and reshaped by the proximity of friendly powers, by a home such as he had never known, by peace, quietude and faith in the recreative forces of his nature:

"Beloved child, your letter—I write you this before I've finished reading it, to tell you it's come, to tell you I can't read it at one draught, so much does it stir my heart. I had to stop when I came to your words about flowers. When we stride into the sea-wind, we think we can draw it whole into our lungs, and suddenly we can breathe no more. What is one to do with infinity? It is as though I heard the language of men for the first time. You see, I know it only from the great eternal poems and from my own struggling efforts—I never found it wonderful in others. Oh, how you make me love language! We speak to each other as the stars speak to the earth, or the earth to the stars, only it is not silence, not the silence of the heavenly bodies, but language, the language of men and women. . . . I am so drawn towards you that I must do something definite for you, something visible and demonstrable, and that will be to take this letter through a morning whose grey skyey indecision is now clearing to my little post-office, which seems infinitely trustworthy now that you have come to know it a little.

"(Later) Now, in one of the loveliest chestnut-avenues on earth (oh, who has ever felt deeply enough what that means?), where I am walking up and down this morning almost alone, I have finished reading your letter with a rich, an infinite feeling that my sense and knowledge of you continue after it is ended; I raise my eyes and lo, where should I not find you, you lovely meaning of the world, who will lead me on to the loftier meanings of the universe, as yet uncomprehended? Oh, it is like a spring of water in my heart; near by lies my old, deep, sulky well—let it—I draw no water there these days.

"I don't know what is happening to me; I pass it a little shyly; a bush of wild roses hides me from it—with what sweet vigour it throws out its shoots!—I turn and kneel, and my spring leaps into my hands. . . . But what have I been writing? I only want to speak of the place round which our first earthly plans can go on circling, loosely related. It should, shall, can and must be whatever place you choose. . . . You wrote 'eighteen days', it is already less—a whole day each day—and you let me hope that in Berlin we can do something different, communal, our own. Love, I don't think of all that yet, I merely carry it at the foundation of my every thought. . . ."

Daily I walked as in a dream through the streets of Grunewald, past gardens where the rose-trees were still swathed, where the first flowers were in bloom beside the last melting snows. I went to the post-office where I handed in my letters to Paris and thought with a leaping heart: another sixteen days, another fourteen, another nine . . .

Then came a letter that contained so much fear and despair that it almost finished everything:

". . . I must tell you all the evil I find in myself, all the falsehood, pettiness, malice and spiritual coarseness; above all, the coarseness, for it is as though a voice were there from my earliest childhood which will not accept its presence in me and strikes out, at random. It would be terrible if you should ever have the shadow of a thought that I am capable of clumsiness, stupidity, brutality—and above all on those floating, winged levels, where brutality no longer exists, whither it rises like an apparition, causing startled glances and disbelief. . . . Oh, if I speak to you of it, near one, just once, of this sickness that pierces deep into the soul and spreads along the whole body, this sense of distortion, like something bent to uses for which it was never intended; a tool notched or rusted or left lying where it cannot be found. And imagine, dear heart, that this befalls it at a moment when it feels sharp, straight, so to speak, prepared . . . now let the master come—Oh, the expectancy in a good tool! Oh, the anticipatory joy in the hammer before the first hammer-blow! And then the tool was put away, carried in dark tool-bags, brought out and regarded with inquisitive eyes, that did not know its purpose; then used wrongly, handled wrongly, till it cut the hands of the users. And they grew angry and threw it in a corner. And it lay there. And strange things were heaped on it. . . . Oh, Benvenuta, there are angels round you in your music; there are angels round you in your joy; there are angels round you in the purity of your mind; perhaps they do much for your sake. Perhaps all your angels stand round the muffled angel of the tool and speak to it . . ."

There they came again, inscrutable forces of destruction that repeatedly mastered him. He had no defence against them; he felt their approach in the midst of his most ardent longing for salvation and security. What comfort I sent him then I do not know, but his answering letter was suffused with new hope:

". . . Oh, Benvenuta, I believe you when I read your letters. Rescuing heart, why else would you have come? O love, O influence that transcends a separation that will soon be ended! How often something hangs over me—the chill of an alien fate. And now how often may there be invisible conflict, high in the air, between your promptings and the inrush of distractions. Not enough that you give me the earth and many countries inimical to me, you must overcome what opposes me high in space. For he who is not pure has enmities everywhere and is not safe from them. Only the pure pass straight through the enemy and unnerve him. . . . We know we love each other from an antiquity before the world was, from the childhood of all ages of life; we love each other from primal being, as stars would love if they were conscious of their glory. And now I know too why I wished not to arouse any feelings towards you but those of my most intuitive childhood, why I seek there for the purest heart-rays to gather them for you, for power, Benvenuta, an unconquerable power of the heart, by which my power towards God shall first begin to be . . ."

Now it was only four days, three—and then came the telegram:

"TOMORROW—RAINER".

On the day before Rilke's arrival in Berlin I was invited to a big party. I went there only to lull my restless heart. Has patience limits when one can think, "Only another twenty-four hours"? All I remember is that I was sitting at dinner next to an important industrialist, who talked of duties on grain and taxes on brandy. He remarked that music was "fun". Then we drank champagne and later on, when the young people began dancing, a woman took me home in her car.

At home I went to my writing-desk without lighting the lamp. Yes, there was the letter, Rilke's last letter before our meeting. I touched the paper of the envelope; I folded my hands over it. If one can pray without words, then that moment of mute devotion was a fervent prayer of thanks. I opened the window and breathed the cold night air from the dark, sleeping garden. As I closed the window I thought, as though in a dream, Flowers from Rainer?

Inside it was warm and still; there was a scent of fresh violets; a kindly hand had put them there for me in a silver bowl on the table. Then, by the light of a little lamp, which made the room glow with golden dusk, I read Rilke's last letter. And there, mysteriously bound up with my thoughts, was the answer to my ardent wish for flowers from Rainer:

". . . You have flowers—I'm glad you told me—on your breakfast table. Yes, your yellow tulips, dear heart; I longed to know whether you had flowers, and was almost on the point of getting Franziska Bruck to send you some roses. . . . I desisted for several reasons, chiefly because I asked myself what, after all, there is of me in such roses, even if I suggest to Franziska Bruck that they are to be of such and such a kind. She has them or she hasn't, and in the end she acts according to my so-called wish, just as her ambition, her zeal and her curiosity dictate. But are they then *my* roses? Doesn't everything bloom for you, my mysterious one? Are not all these your flowers that I write of— not one that you have not engendered, sun, sun of the heart? And how many more, for which my plot is too small, do you summon and summon, you radiant voice. It would go hard with a botanist, for they all bear your name and how should he find his way among them? They are like the stars of heaven, which in truth have only heaven's own unutterable names, and not those we give them."

I held his gift of these words in my hands, I thought I could not bear so much happiness. I hardly dared read on.

But then, then the dark powers called again for my beloved voice of solace—and a sinister, foreboding fate made him say:

". . . I shall see you, Benvenuta, with unready eyes; my hands, my hands of yesterday, will take refuge in yours. . . . Benvenuta, what does one do on the eve of such a day? How does one spend the night in order to be worthy of the coming morn? Will a dream come and spoil me for you, as happened today in the first light of dawn, when you took me by the hand in a forest? It was a forest of tall trees; it rose gently between the trunks and the earth was a quite metallic green from the moist, growing leaves. Further up was a great tree that broke into branches at the top of its long, still poise; behind it the path still rose, but round the tree was a faint, golden, vaporous sheen that sucked the interior of the forest into it. I wanted to take this path, but then —you passed it, softly and quickly. I looked where you were, in another direction, but I cannot remember what it was like. Oh, Benvenuta, dearest, near one, nearest, perhaps as soon as you touch me you will feel that the flaw can no longer be mended, that no tone comes even from the surest touch, because a dark, pitiless destiny clings somewhere at the base of the bell. Then *tell* me, dear heart . . . take it seriously, take it hard, in your heart, most sacred to me. . . .

"The repose of childhood, youth's toughening exercise and the unviolated future: the night of the squire before his consecration to knighthood was precisely at the point of intersection of the radiations of those three forces; therefore in that night the young men became strong and transparent and of rich potential. But where is the repose of my childhood, and how can it help me— my long since violated future? One thing I want: to watch and pray the night before I see you, Benvenuta, to lie on my knees fasting, as though I never needed nourishment—upheld at all points by my expectancy, by your approach. . . .

"RAINER"

Meeting

DUSK was falling. I went on foot all the way like a pilgrim to a shrine. I traversed what seemed to me a hundred streets, went through avenues, through a little park by the river, where the trees were hardly less bare than in winter—and then on again past long rows of houses. Tram-cars rattled past, cars and pedestrians drifted by like phantoms. "Marburger-strasse 4," I thought; and there was no other thought in my mind but that sober address. When at last I reached the house and saw over the door a plate, "*Hospiz des Westens*", illuminated by an electric light, I could have gone no farther. I clung to the door-handle. It was some time before I rang. My voice almost failed me as I asked the maidservant who opened the door whether Herr Rilke had arrived and was staying there.

The girl, who wore a blue-and-white striped dress and a white cap, answered with cool politeness: "Yes. The third floor, please. Room 24."

I went up broad, carpeted stairs and past many doors. It was deathly quiet; only the gas-burners on the stairs made a strange, hissing sound—and there was Room 24, its door in the full glare of the light, exactly opposite the head of the stairs.

I stood still for some time: I did not knock till I heard someone coming up from downstairs. For the length of a heartbeat no one answered, then I heard, "Yes?"—nervous, interrogatory. It was the voice I had always known, the dear, dear, ardently awaited voice. I went in.

As though through a mist I saw a spacious room. In one corner by the windows was a small, green-shaded writing-lamp; there was no other light; and before me stood Rainer Maria, a slim, dark, almost pathetic figure. His blue eyes looked into mine; I had never seen such a shining, unearthly face.

"Benvenuta—at last, at last you have come," he said. And I thought that the loving tone of that voice could cause me to forget all else, close my eyes and listen to it for ever.

Then we were holding each other's hands; we sat on the little green velvet sofa, looked at each other and laughed and cried.

"I have just written to you," he said. "I couldn't help it: it was still too unbelievable that you would actually come. . . ." We were silent again, as though afraid of shattering that happy dream.

"I must go on looking at you," he said. "Yes, it is you; it is really you. First I thought your hair was brown but it had to be auburn." And I thought, "He is not a man. He is an apparition that has come by a miracle to our poor earth and me."

I did not foresee that later on that thought was to bring us unspeakable suffering. All was clear, bright and holy in our silence and in all our talk. We forgot time. We had so infinitely much to say that we might never have written each other all those letters. The world was as though new created; we walked about in it, astonished, forgetting the hours.

When I left, Rilke accompanied me part of the way. "*Auf Wiedersehen* tomorrow," was his leave-taking and there was so much happiness in his voice that I thought of his first letter from Paris—"All the flags are flying."

When I reached home everyone was asleep. I passed quietly through the dark vestibule. In my room I went over to a large mirror and looked at myself. I felt my face was new and sanctified, for now I had looked with my mortal eyes on an immortal spirit. I had with me Rainer's letter, written in the train and in his room after his arrival. I unfolded it and read. At the end he had written a poem for me:

> "Oh, I went through the thickets like a breeze,
> escaped like gusty smoke from every roof;
> where others found in custom joy and ease
> like a strange custom I remained aloof.
> my hands went forward fearfully
> into the fateful clasp of other hands;
> in that outpouring every heart expands,
> and I could but myself outpouréd be.
>
> "You see, we need a foothold in the dust
> even to gaze upon the planet's track,
> for trust can only come of others' trust,

all giving is no more than giving back.
the night asked nought of me; but if I peer
up to the firmament bestarred,
the marred to the eternally unmarred,
whereon stand I? Am I here?

"Streams toward me into my darkened way
your heart's warm orbit? Little time endures,
only a little time, and I shall lay
with gentleness my own poor hands in yours.
since they were last at rest how long has passed!
say, can you feel what all the years have meant
that I a stranger among strangers went?
and now you take me home at last!"[1]

My last conscious thought before falling asleep was this:
If Death came now, it could not destroy me, for it would bear
into eternity a spirit completely fulfilled.

[1] Unpublished original in the possession of the author:
        "Ach, wie Wind durchging ich die Gesträuche,
        jedem Haus entdrang ich wie ein Rauch,
        wo sich andre freuten in Gebräuche
        blieb ich strenge wie ein fremder Brauch.
        Meine Hände gingen schreckhaft ein
        in der andern schicksalvolle Schliessung;
        alle, alle mehrte *die Ergiessung:*
        und ich konnte nur vergossen sein.

        "Siehst du, selbst um das Gestirn zu schauen,
        brauchts ein kleines irdisches Beruhn,
        denn Vertrauen kommt nur aus Vertrauen,
        alles Wohltun ist ein Wiedertun;
        ach, die Nacht verlangte nichts von mir,
        doch wenn ich mich zu den Sternen kehrte
        der Versehrte an das Unversehrte:
        Worauf stand ich? War ich hier?

        "Flutet mir in diese trübe Reise
        Deines Herzens warme Bahn entgegen?
        Nur noch Stunden und ich werde leise
        meine Hände in die Deinen legen.
        Ach, wie lange ruhten sie nicht aus.
        Kannst Du Dir denn denken, dass ich Jahre
        so—ein Fremder unter Fremden fahre
        und nun endlich nimmst Du mich nach Haus".

Reality

(*From My Berlin Diary*)

Grunewaldhaus.

March, 1914.

THE snow on the lawn has melted. When I opened my window this morning, the scent of the first violets came in on the mild spring air. Above the trees in the garden was the light, pale-blue morning sky, and blue and yellow crocuses are in flower beside the gravel path that leads to the gate.

When I went into the garden after breakfast, Rainer was standing outside the iron gate, and it seemed so completely natural for him to be standing there in his grey coat and dark, soft hat that he might have stood there every morning for years, pressed the little yellow button of the bell and waited to be admitted.

In the cool spring sunshine he looked slighter and smaller than in his room last night. The colour of his eyes is a remarkably clear blue; his narrow face seems to glow from inside as though a spiritual fire could make him flare up or die down. We shook hands and smiled at each other without speaking. How much joy there is in his face and how much pain! I cannot help thinking again and again that the destinies of all humanity are revealed and reflected in his eyes and in his almost too big, expressive mouth.

No, he did not want to come in; would I go for a walk with him or—he looked at me inquiringly, almost frightened, ". . . I have found a work-room, quite near, just one room. I should like to take it. You can hardly imagine *how beautiful it is* . . ."

"Then we will go at once and look at it together."

We were in such a hurry to see the new room that we ran down the avenue to Bismarck-platz.

"I hope it's still there—that is, of course, there for me—though I shouldn't be surprised if we found such a beautiful room had suddenly vanished for good, as happens in dreams." No, it was still there and, as we entered it, it seemed indeed like a room in a dream.

"We'll call it the Andersen room," I said, delighted. "No other name is good enough for it." Rainer did not answer; he merely nodded and went happily from one piece of furniture to another, examining the brightly-polished cherry-wood chairs, upholstered in pastel-blue damask, the bookcase with green silk curtains over each pane of glass, the writing-desk, standing square in front of the wide double window, the old coloured etchings in little gilt frames on the soft flowered wallpaper. It reeked of cleanliness. There were soft, white curtains at the windows, which looked out on trees and, in the distance, far-away forests. In a cabinet were painted cups, a tea-pot, bright *biedermeier* plates and fine old glass. Nothing had been forgotten; there were even flowers on the round table—a dark blue bowl of primulas and anemones.

"To be able to work here, read with you, hold good talk and——" Rainer stopped with big, expectant, almost incredulous eyes. I understood: "—and play Beethoven, Bach, Schumann and everything that's beautiful."

"You know," he cried happily. "But how will you do it?"

"I'm going to Ibach's—that's a big piano firm—to ask them to send you up a grand piano. Today!"

Rainer came across to me from the window. He had become quite serious. "How do you do all that so simply, so simply, without thinking of it—like breathing or sleeping? The strange thing is, I'm taking it all for granted. I must tell you that a big part of my mind is taken up with wondering; I wonder at towers and cathedrals, at the stars always—and at my own life. But I don't wonder at you—I close my eyes in you. But, how am I to warn you quickly of my incapacity for music?"

"Simply have confidence in it and listen. You can do that, can't you?"

"I can do it? I don't know. And even if some day I can, people won't believe me. Once an acquaintance dragged me off to a big concert full of noisy people; the buzz and banging of doors hurt me—then they played a Beethoven symphony: gigantic happenings burst suddenly over those people who had been so noisy and now sat still as if they knew. . . . I must have

c

stared stiffly in front of me, for my acquaintance said to me between two movements, 'Shut your eyes and open your ears!' "

I looked at Rilke, horrified at such crude presumption, and he went on: "I don't know whether I ever told you that I seemed to be able to endure music only in churches, where it went straight up to God, rising into the arches of the roof. One felt it did not stay with the people but streamed through them: it cared nothing for us, it belonged to God and God only. Tell me, did you really feel familiar with it as a child? Did you pass between the lions and angels of music, sure that it would do you no harm?"

"I can't tell you; I can only play it. You will hear it."

Later we drove together into the town, where we parted, Rilke to fetch his luggage, I to go to Ibach's. There I tried the pianos. One, a grand, pleased me particularly, and I chose it for the Andersen room. They promised to send it early the same afternoon. At midday I drove back to Grunewald. At Bismarck-platz I looked up at Rainer's windows. They were open: the white curtains fluttered in a faint wind, but I could see no one.

Does he really live up there, close to where I'm staying? Is this dream real? I asked myself, and I could not help smiling, full of gratitude and happiness. ". . . I don't wonder at you—I close my eyes in you."

This has been for me a wonderful and unforgettable day. The piano has come. It stands at an angle to the big double window in the Andersen room; to its right is the desk and a little farther from the window a wide chaise-longue with a beautiful rug over it. Rilke calls this room the three in one—work, rest and music.

Rainer has let me play to him here for the first time. It was a warm, late afternoon after long continuing rain. When I came in the window was open and the room full of the smell of the fresh, wet earth. Outside there are buds on the trees and the bushes in the garden have put on their first tender green. I filled a little vase with water and put some snowdrops and violets on the writing-desk. Rainer, who was just sealing a letter, looked up and placed his hand on my arm. "Oh, thank you, dear. Will you be patient just for a moment? First the daily business, then I can be really with you."

I sat down at the window and looked out into the failing light. Outside, a blackbird was singing, loud and flute-like, and it was as though the bird's voice filled the room with sweet perfume.

Rilke had closed his brief-case and cleared away the papers. "Do you remember," he asked, "what you wrote me once about the *Meistersinger?*—That the finest moment for you is when the theatre is darkened and the conductor lifts his baton. Not a note has yet been lost; it all lies before you—that is what you wrote. Oh, Benvenuta, to think that there was a time when life lay before one like that, in all its abundance—and now you are going to play in this room. Is it possible that your music will bring order again to my inner life, as I have so often dreamed? Tell me—am I *too* presumptuous?"

I had sat down at the piano and laid my fingers on the keys. My heart was fluttering; I felt as though I was about to conduct some holy rite, to bring music for the first time to a man—no, to an immortal soul—who was waiting for it.

Then the notes of the piano rang out. It has a warm tone that seems to fill the room with mild light. I played a theme of Händel's, a simple, tender melody, then an aria by Bach. I felt I must not alarm him with the impact of a flood of notes, and so at first I played only simple melodies, a little song by Schumann, a pastorale by Scarlatti. And all the time the blackbird's song sounded through my music, the spring-voice of a coming season.

When the piano fell silent darkness had fallen. The blackbird sang no more and the stillness was long and deep. Then I felt that Rainer had come up noiselessly behind me; I felt his hands on my hair and his hot face against my cheek, streaming with tears. We spoke no more; we walked through the rain-wet evening, past quiet gardens, to my house. In that hour my life received the blessing of God. When we parted, Rainer took my face between his two hands and kissed me on the forehead.

Rilke has been to see us at Grunewald. He has established a sincere friendship with Frau Delbrück, just as I had hoped. Who could fail to love him, and who could withstand the magic of that rare, motherly woman? It was delightful to see them together, and Rilke felt so much at home with us that his behaviour to the whole party was quite unconstrained, as though he had known us all for some time.

Two of the Delbrück children were there, Betti and Theo, a few young girls, and Ferruccio Busoni's elder son, Benni, a radiantly handsome boy. Frau Delbrück told us a very strange story from her own life and showed us an etching by Max Klinger, which, she said, very few people know and which was connected with her story. It was a delightful, happy evening. Rilke did not say very much and he sat some distance away from me, but we were very close because of a wonderful, inner understanding. Sometimes I believe he knows one's thoughts; he often replies to unspoken questions, with a kind of wary naturalness that is characteristic of him. The children love him. Betti sometimes put her little hand on his arm and he smiled at her, which made her blush with pleasure. When we parted Benni asked me if we were going to the *Philharmonie* on Tuesday —Busoni was playing Beethoven's concerto in E-flat major. I have already got tickets, and told Benni that I should like to introduce Rilke to Busoni. Benni said his father would be delighted; he admires Rilke's work and calls him the "musician of words".

Afternoon in the Andersen room.

I got some little cakes and apples, laid the table prettily and made the tea. Rainer is very grateful for such attentions. "A man should never know where a meal comes from," he said, half joking. But I know he finds it an effort to go out and buy the things he needs.

We talked a good deal about the approaching concert. He wanted to know what Busoni looks like, so I described his appearance, his home, his splendid wife, his life in Vienna with his pupils. Rilke is eagerly looking forward to hearing him. All of a sudden he has "so much courage for music" . . . "A short time ago I read Busoni's 'Æsthetics of Music'[1]" he said. "I thought it excellent; and I admired the way he writes German— perfect in itself and amazing when you remember that he is a Latin."

I told him that no one can play Bach and Beethoven better or more "germanly", except perhaps Casals. I have often had the pleasure of playing with Casals and he is a Latin too. We went on to talk of great men and their destinies, then Rainer re- membered that he had asked Frau Delbrück to write down her story about Klinger. I had brought it with me. Rainer read it

[1] *Aesthetik der Tonkunst.*

aloud, and we re-lived in spirit the following poignant incident:

"My friends, this evening I showed you an etching by Klinger that you had not seen before—the white-clad figure of a dead man lying at full length on a bed. The face, full of deep tranquility and relief, appeared to you to have entered with blessed faith into its eternal sleep. You asked me who it was. It was Klinger's best friend, a man who loved art above all things, who served artists with all the vigour of the love he bore their work, and who could detect the true artist with unfailing certainty. Klinger, he and I had known each other for years. We often travelled together; hardly an autumn passed without our meeting in Italy. Once we went to Rome together and, soon after our arrival, paid a visit to Frascati and stayed there a week. Every day we walked up to Tusculum, whence we could see the Mediterranean gleaming like a narrow strip of silver beyond the *campagna*. Klinger did a good deal of sketching. He planned to illustrate the *Odyssey*, and we had to read Homer aloud to him. Those were happy days. One morning we returned to Rome and when I left Klinger and his friend, who was in particularly good spirits, I arranged to meet them at their villa that afternoon and go to the Palazzo Borghese. Tired by our drive through the hot, sunny countryside, I fell asleep after lunch and did not wake till the clock over the fireplace was striking five. I hurried out. Klinger lived only a few streets away.

"The gate of the little villa was unlocked. I went up the steps, surprised to find all the doors open. I shouted, went in, crossed the first room. No one answered and I felt a sudden indescribable alarm. I went into the second room. A motionless figure, wrapped in white linen, was lying there on the bed. The face, full of unearthly calm, wore a strange, remote smile—it was the face of Klinger's friend, who had been so cheerful and gay when I left him only a few hours before. And then I saw Klinger too. He was sitting quite still, his pencil in his hand, his eyes, almost extinguished with grief, fixed on the dead man—and he was drawing.

"Gradually I realised what had happened; I understood that, sitting there petrified with grief, yet still a creative artist, he was rendering his last homage to the dead by using him as a model for the poignant work I showed you today."

"What a splendid death!" said Rilke with emotion. "How

empty of jealousy he must have been in his eternal sleep, for all
the comings and goings and all the grief of others."

Later he went on to speak of one of the fundamental ideas of
his life—that everyone should have the death that belonged to
him and was commensurate with him and had been developing
in him all his life. "In Florence, in Bologna, in Venice, in Rome,
wherever I have been I have stood beside the gravestones, a
student of death, and have let *them* teach me. I have looked out
for them in all countries and it seemed to me touchingly
magnanimous that those who died young had taken time to love
a girl and not been afraid that the expenditure would be too great
for the little time they had."

Yesterday evening in the *Philharmonie*. I was anxious about
the effect the great hall, the many strange people and above all
Busoni's playing would have on Rilke. Busoni is always a new
and unpredictable experience. I can imagine that those hearing
him for the first time are shocked, almost overwhelmed, by the
might of his genius. His playing is always like fate, the purest
affirmation, flight into higher spheres, outcry and silence, the
ardour of all living, overflowing jubilance and passionate prayer.
I asked myself, would Rilke be able to bear it, would his shy
nature be equal to the suddenness of the experience? My
timidity was wonderfully put to shame. I do not know which
was the finer—Busoni's playing or Rilke's listening.

It seemed as though these two very different natures com-
plemented each other in a perfect reciprocity. Once, during an
orchestral interlude when the piano was silent, Busoni glanced
across at us, greeted me with his eyes and gave Rilke the attention he reserves for people in whom he is spontaneously
interested. He had no idea who was sitting beside me—Benni
had told him nothing—but he must have realised at one glance
what an extraordinary person Rilke is.

A foolish little episode occurred during the adagio. It an-
noyed me at the time but had a charming sequel. An old lady
sitting behind me began to make a loud rustling noise with silver
paper during a marvellous pianissimo passage on the piano. She
rummaged in her silk handbag and was not at all put out even
when I turned and gave her a reproving look. At the interval I
said to Rilke: "It is quite incomprehensible how people can

make a noise with silver paper when someone is playing. What lack of consideration both for the artist and the audience!''

The concert was over, and while waves of applause burst through the hall, the old lady rose, made me a delightful bow and said: "I am really most grateful to you for the lesson you gave me. My name is Schultheiss, and I live at 6, Dörnberg-strasse. Will you give me the pleasure of being my guest at dinner to-morrow? I should like very much to get to know you better. D'Albert will be there and Marteau, probably Marie von Bunsen and a few other interesting people.''

Now it was my turn to apologise, but the old lady would have none of it and we parted with a warm *auf Wiedersehen*. I almost fell on her neck!

This morning with Rainer in the Tiergarten. We talked about the concert. He thinks Busoni incomparably fine, and made some wonderful remarks about Beethoven. ". . . how deeply I understood that Beethoven had to be solitary to create such works. For his music's sake even the last criterion—his hearing —was taken from him so that he could surge like the primeval forest and forget the possibility of being the other, who listens to the forest and is afraid . . .''

We were pleased too with Frau Schultheiss and her chocolates, which had led to such a welcome acquaintanceship. Rilke was enchanted with the incident, and when I confessed that I had really behaved quite rudely, he was almost angry: "I think it was all right and fitting! Like a celestial sum it comes out without remainder. And it was so good when she told you her name, as though, with all the authority of her years and position, she were calling in the whole family to help her look into it and make you reparation and apology. Believe me, Benvenuta, if only people would look at each other straight out of their deepest splendour, full of joy or anger, one after the other would be shocked into naming his name and would be changed. But, as it is, how do they look at each other? And so all the balls chink together or the chocolates or whatever they have in their meagre bags, which are very welcome to the name of 'ridicules' . . .''

Dear Rainer, I shall not be there when you come to have lunch with us tomorrow. Forgive me, but I must go very early to

Potsdam and shall probably stay there the whole day. Dr. B. is there and we have to come to an arrangement about the Hamburg concert. He does not want a modern programme; he would like me to play Beethoven's G-major. I think of all the splendid things you have said about Beethoven and I shall study and play him now in quite a different way. I will gladly give up the Tschaikovsky; that is only a piece of *bravura*, and it rushes away in the last movement with true Slav irresponsibility. I would only have played it to oblige Dr. B., but now everything is to be altered: first the Coriolanus overture, then the piano concerto and finally the Eroica—a whole evening of Beethoven—I talked to d'Albert about it yesterday and he thinks it a very good programme.

It is very late now (or rather early, for it is past midnight) but I must just tell you about the evening at Frau S's (if only you had been there!). Her flat is very handsome but quite jolly—flowers everywhere, good pictures on the walls, the whole thing artistic. It was a big party. In addition to d'Albert, of whom I shall tell you more later, I got to know Marteau, Lola Kirschner (Osipp Schubin) and a great grand-niece of Schubert, Frau Geissler. And someone else—but this is going to be uncanny, Rainer, and you won't understand it at first. When we were going in to dinner an imposing old gentleman in mufti arrived. I did not catch his name when we were introduced, but he sat exactly opposite me. I looked at him and thought, "If I did not know very well that Wildenbruch is dead, I would swear he is sitting there in front of me."

Suddenly someone said to him, "I assure you, Herr von Wildenbruch——" What do *you* say to that? Theo told me only the other day that he was one of the delegation of students that walked behind Wildenbruch's coffin, and here was Wildenbruch in the flesh, being treated with the deference befitting a poet, and no one seemed to find anything odd about it.

I plucked up my courage and engaged him in conversation across the table. My mysterious *vis-à-vis* proved to be very well read; he talked at length of literature, knew all about it and was very pleased to hear that I had attended a performance of the *Rabensteinerin*.

"A few scenes have been re-written," he said, "and I think the piece is all the better for it."

On the way home I ran into Theo, who had been to the theatre. Instead of returning his greeting, I said, "Theo, you're mistaken. Wildenbruch is still alive."

Theo looked at me quite horrified. "What has put that idea into your head? I was at his funeral."

"That is quite possible," I said in despair, "but all the same I've just had dinner with him. He was pleased to hear I know the *Rabensteinerin*, and told me he had re-written several scenes in it!"

"You ought to go and lie down," said Theo, and his voice had suddenly become noticably gentle. "I'll fetch mother."

Frau Delbrück came quickly in a beautiful lilac wrap (she had been just going to bed, poor dear), and I told her the whole story. She listened attentively and handed me over to Hedwig. Hedwig is her trusty maid; she has no sense of humour and took me off like a stubborn child to my room. There she put a cold compress on my forehead and treated me as if I was seriously ill.

Meanwhile Frau Schultheiss had been fetched out of bed to answer the telephone. Half asleep at first and then with great amusement, she gave an assurance that I was quite right in the head. I had mistaken General Ludwig von Wildenbruch for his dead brother, the writer, Ernst von Wildenbruch, whom however he resembles as one pea another. We all laughed so much that I am far too wide awake to get to sleep and had to write and tell you all about it.

In a few hours I shall drive past your house and you will still be asleep. I send you a thousand warm greetings and wish you a happy day. The rose tree you sent me yesterday evening has opened all its buds. They are a tender pink like the first glow of sun in the morning. Thank you for everything, dear one!

(Betti will deliver this letter on her way to school. She is very proud of being allowed to bring you something. I send you also the Beethoven letters you wanted, in the Kastner edition.)

The Busonis have invited Rainer and me to dinner on Sunday.

Today with Rilke in the Grunewald. We walked a long way, past little lakes. Rainer remembered the pictures by Leistikow, who discovered much simple beauty in this rather dreary landscape. We saw a deer crossing a forest path. It took to flight as soon as it caught sight of us. Then we talked of blood-sports. I thought that Rilke—like myself—would be a passionate opponent of shooting, but he understood it, though he is a great lover of animals. That is to say, he knows the power atavism exerts on men, and explained to me that cruelty and the desire to kill are also, as he said, "hospitably at home" deep in man's nature. Many people struggle against this instinct or allow it to become dwarfed out of fear or indolence or "God knows what near or distant reasons," while others foster it in their own way, though it be only to hunt and kill animals. The instinct of hunger, from which sprang the primitive beginnings of all blood-sports, developed later into a power-instinct. In India, however, religion forbade the eating of meat. Hundreds of thousands, millions, obey this command, which is a command of love—love of their supreme God and of the animals which are God's creatures.

I said that when one talks with a hunter he always ends by assuring one that he loves animals and finds pleasure not in the actual killing but in the morning mood of the woods, in observing and preserving game, that shooting is only a sort of duty. To which I always reply that, if there is no pleasure in killing, one could leave it to the men who slaughter cattle.

Rilke smiled, but his eyes were still sad. "You see," he said, "all that is said about 'love' of animals is true and at the same time untrue. People feel they owe these shifts and subterfuges to themselves, for who can be certain that he is true? Yes, who even *knows* what 'true' means? And if one does know, who has the courage to be true and to be cruel, or, at least, the courage to think every thought, even the most horrible, even the basest? The only thing that matters is that such a thought does not become, so to speak, *valid* in the mind; that it does not tempt one; that such a thought is confined to its own level and never allowed even to guess how things are in the forecourts of the heart and in the eternally valid laws of goodness, of life in purity and in community with nature. But, after all, what do we know?" he concluded, sighing. "Fundamentally does not everything reach out beyond us, beyond our innermost and our least? Has not everything around us in the world law and validity even without us?"

Sunday at Busoni's.

No one who has once seen this beautiful home could ever

forget it. No. 11, Viktoria-Luise-platz is like many other build-
ings in Berlin, but once you have ascended to the third floor and
rung the doorbell, you have a unique and delightful experience—
that of stepping out of the dark vestibule into the music-room.
The music-room had two big black Bechstein grands, standing
side by side, and above them, with a green velvet curtain on the
wall behind it, a gold Buddha. In the curve of the window was a
bench with cushions and, opposite, a cupboard and a few easy
chairs. Next door was the library. This beautiful room was
panelled in wood; great built-in cupboards full of costly things
reached to the ceiling—first editions, splendid leather-bound
volumes, Spanish literature, E. T. A. Hoffmann, Balzac, Goethe,
Ariosto, Dante, the culture of all countries and continents. On
tables were the new books, art journals, piles of periodicals.

Busoni was just coming down from the "tower", where his
workroom is situated. He welcomed Rilke with a warmth
which had in it a delightful Latin quality of veneration. To see
the two men shake hands was like witnessing the meeting of two
worlds—the musician, who is present and future, "always a
new beginning", as he says of himself—and the poet who
follows the trail of the past ("childhood—whither can it have
gone?"); Busoni all fire and spirit, affirming life, a ready laugher,
childlike and superstitious; Rilke, shy, constrained, full of grave,
apprehensive knowledge of life, profound and quiet, with a
humour that shines out only occasionally; Busoni rejecting all
that is withered and past, a man inwardly full of youth who
lives with young people; Rilke portraying the transient, the poor,
the rejected, knowing the sorrows of all created things and also
the bliss of overcoming, of creation.

But these two antagonistic men were united by the knowledge
of a reverence for their respective vocations and by their understanding of life. That was clear from the warmth with which they
shook hands, and they immediately became friends.

Frau Busoni joined us and we sat down to luncheon. There
were spring flowers and green wine-glasses on the beautifully
laid table, the "round table that is always too small". Busoni
unfolded his napkin and as the soup was served, he said merrily,
"Today we are having a special pudding—Viennese *Wuchteln*."
He had obtained the recipe in Vienna for this popular dish and
every cook he had was compelled to learn it. Busoni took a

special delight in serving it to guests from Austria. Talk about
Metternich and the Great Coalition did not spoil this pudding.
It was delicious. The *Powidl* with which it was filled was a gift
from friends in Bohemia.

After the meal black coffee was served in the library and the
conversation turned to Marcel Proust and his new book, *Du côté
de chez Swann*. Busoni thought it good though a little too long.
Rilke did not quite agree. "I find the second part, in spite of
some fine flashes, almost boring, often just fiction, one of those
things the French cannot help producing, sometimes from the
left, sometimes from the right," he said. "Only the passages
towards the end about the phrase in the sonata, and the music he
strikes now and then at unrelated intervals on the innumerable
keys of the universe—only these passages perhaps are of great
importance in all those crowded pages. Admittedly the book's
shortcomings are balanced by a hundred virtues, which,
differentiated in tones and half-tones, extend from the merely
amusing to the really significant."

Afterwards Rilke asked about Busoni's "New Æsthetics of
Music". He was especially interested in the possibilities of an
extended system of quarter tones. We talked for a long time
about old and new theories, about the *Brautwahl*, Busoni's
plans for opera and the text of "Turandot". Finally, when
Busoni mentioned that he was particularly fond of the *Song of the
Sea* from Rilke's *New Poems*, Rilke recited it to us. He spoke it
freely from memory with a restrained inner fire, as only he can
speak. Unforgettable to me is his quiet, inclined face, the tone of
his voice, recreating the poem afresh—verses that are at once
music and picture.

> "Primeval breath from sea
>   sea-wind by night . . ."[1]

He spoke it with such fervour that one caught the salt tang of the
sea and the nocturnal storm:

> "pure space
>   rushing from realms unknown."[2]

[1] From "Song of the Sea" from "Requiem and Other Poems", translated
by J. B. Leishman.
    The original German is as follows:
    Uraltes Wehn vom Meer,
    Meerwind bei Nacht. . . .
[2] Ibid. *lauter Raum reissend von weit herein. . . . .*

And with what restrained jubilation the poem ends:
> "O how keenly known—
> moonlit clinging-place,
> wakening fig-tree's moan." [1]

Busoni sat still, leaning a little forward, absorbed in listening.
Not much more was said. We left soon after, for other guests
were expected that evening. Two men, two worlds, understood
one another.

Frau Busoni said at the door when we bade her good-bye:
"Ferruccio has enjoyed it *so* much."

Rainer, Frau Delbrück and I were at the *Lyzeum-klub* this
afternoon, where I was playing. Rainer sat, completely unnoticed and unrecognised, among the old ladies (". . . the
three grim women on the sofa were terrifying, a group out of
Tartarus," he said later, quite unnerved), enjoying the tea and his
incognito. Previously the *Cornet* had been read, not well and not
badly, and afterwards one of the "grim women" said to Rainer:
"I should like to know what the author of a modern epic like that
really looks like."

Rainer replied with humour and complete self-assurance, for
which I admired him greatly: "Poets usually look different from
what one expects."—"How do you mean? Do you know him?
Where does he live? Is he young?"

Now there was no holding them. Three girls and one of the
"grim" women joined us and began to ask questions. Frau
Delbrück bravely swallowed her laughter with a sandwich and I
managed with some difficulty to turn the conversation to modern
writers in general and Frank Wedekind in particular. And when
the curious ladies had begun to gnaw the new bone, Rilke quietly
slipped away. In a pause the "grim" one remarked persistently,
"But I should have liked to hear something about Rilke. Do you
think that gentleman who just left knows him?" I got up, wished
them good afternoon and then released my bolt: "Yes, he knows
Rilke fairly well. You see, he *is* Rilke."

A Signorina Cecilia Braschi sent Rilke her Italian translation

---

[1] Ibid. *Oh, wie fühlt dich ein treibender Feigenbaum, oben im Mondschein.*
The translation of the third extract is rather free: the meaning is,
literally: Oh, how a budding fig-tree feels you, above in the moonlight!—The
Translator.

of the *Cornet*.[1] He read it to me, sitting on the window-seat of the Andersen room. "Well, people are like that," he said, and laughed his dear, light-hearted laugh. "She translates '*Sommerwinde*' as 'convolvolo', little wind, but still there is much good in it—only it is too hasty."

I had brought with me my copy of the *Cornet* and we compared various passages with the translation, which seemed to me to be done with great enthusiasm but too little sense of the finer nuances of Rilke's art. Rainer told me of his own translation of the "Centaur". He had spent weeks and months feeling his way into the spirit of the work, had studied Guerin's mode of expression in order to transplant its essence into the German language, "almost as one sets a flower in new soil, taking care that it goes on blooming there."

The afternoon post came and brought a few letters and a parcel from Göttingen. "You see," said Rilke, pleased, "two people live there, a man and his wife, who have kept a home ready for me almost as long as I can remember, a room that is always prepared and in which no one else ever stays—even my green leather slippers stand ready inside the door—I need only knock whenever I like and I am at home."

The parcel from these friends contained reproductions of several paintings by Magnasco. Rilke did not know them and was so enchanted that he sat for some time absorbed in them. They were strange pictures. A fantastic landscape and a group of ecstatic monks. "You might almost think Greco had painted them," Rilke said.

As we talked he took a note-book out of his desk and read me his notes about El Greco. I asked to be allowed to copy them. They are written on a catalogue of the Prado folded into his note-book, half obliterated words "jotted down in pencil, more seeing than writing," he said. Their subject was the famous "Crucifixion".

". . . in front of the dark, broken skies, the cross with the long, pale flame of His body, and above Him, the detailed inscription, longer than one knows it, as though it were the endless denomination of His sorrows. Mary and John to right and left in the picture, turning away, repeating the direction of His eternally uplifted agony, incapable of more. Only to Mary Magdalene,

[1] *Die Weise von Liebe und Tod des Cornets Christoph Rilke.*

watching the blood stream from His crossed, nailed feet, comes the eagerness to suffer. She throws herself on her knees; she catches the blood flowing down the cross, one grasping hand held close under the feet, and the other, the left hand, far down on the wood; she tries to be the first and the last to catch it—but she has not strength enough. And as she looks up, helpless, through the black flames of the air, she sees it jet from the wound in His breast and gush from the wounds in His hands; she sees nothing but His blood. But an angel has already thrown itself beside her, slantwise, and helps her—and two angels take form, moth-pale, under the dripping hands, up in the night, and float towards the blood as though to embrace it, enraptured, with bare hands, and catch it like music . . ."

Serious talk of the world of genius, of God's gifts and of misunderstandings and then, before I went home, the happiest farewell. Rilke had in front of him my copy of the *Cornet*, and wished to write something in it. "And if you like," he said, "we will go out for a while in the fresh air before you go home to dinner." I told him that unfortunately it was still raining. "No, no, it's not raining now. Look down there—a dog going by without an umbrella."

A little grey pug was trotting down the wet, deserted street. It had a black nose and was making its dignified way towards the front garden of the house opposite. And there was the dedication in my copy of the *Cornet*: "A dog going by without an umbrella".

This year the trees and bushes are growing green before their time; white clouds sail across a clear sky, as though summer were trying to come before March is out. Sparrows chirp in the streets and blackbirds sing in the gardens; even a finch alights sometimes on the little windmill in the garden next door and rehearses its new song. Yesterday evening I read in one of Rainer's long, long letters his description of spring in foreign lands:

". . . for three days there was something of spring in the air here; then, last night, came the full moon and held the universe wide open; cosmic cold streamed in: today it blows and clouds and knows not what it should do. Then your letter came. If only you knew, Benvenuta, that when such a little letter arrives from

you (beautiful was this last one, written out of a single com-
prehensive spirit, as though by moonlight—when there is a moon
again I will read it at the window in my night-black room); when
such a letter comes, you should see, Benvenuta, how I go quite
nervously, with a full, full heart, down the stairs, biting my lower
lip, like children carrying a terribly full cup. Yes, spring! . . .
Formerly spring in Paris was amongst the most wonderful I
knew. . . . Spring in the country is easy, but spring in a town!
I know only two that can bring it off, that have the essence of it,
as though it burst forth everywhere from their bride-pale walls,
as though the windows first catch the invisible in their mirrors
and toss it into the near, tangible world (Rome takes it greatly to
its heart; Rome is stirred; Rome makes a festival; Rome—when
spring comes across the *campagna*, already tired of emotion—
Rome welcomes it, as the father welcomed the prodigal son.)
But I know of only two towns that are permeated by it, so that in
the pavements, in the house-fronts, in the no longer cold
balustrades of the bridges, there is no spot that has not secretly
had news of it, that is not informed, that will not be able tomorrow to give answer to spring's faintest ethereal question, to
any question, any—without mistake—the whole poem; Moscow,
that accepts it as a peasant-child accepts the story of creation,
knowing it well by heart; and Paris, Paris that throws light into
the eyes of spring, like pollen of all enraptured love spent there
since the days of Abelard."

Reality! The days pass in happy, wishless peace. It seems as if
the fear of those internal dæmons had been a dream, a restless
dream before the glad awakening to the knowledge of safety.
Rainer is happy and cheerful, secure and without apprehension.
It is as if he were really resting after a long and strenuous journey.
His eyes have grown brighter, the expression on his face more
vital. The many hours in the woods, by the lakes, in the sun,
have tanned his cheeks. He can laugh so heartily. And even in
serious and weighty talk he remains in the midst of life, without
fear, in a wise composure. Is it possible that he will remain so?
Oh God, is it possible? I dare not think of the future, for every
day of this rich, loving present is a gift from heaven. It is as
though a great and good spirit has descended from the mysterious heavens to bring happiness to the human beings
privileged to see him, often to make us happy by his presence

alone, by his being in the world. A great spirit, though a man
like us, and yet not a man like us. I often reflect on this apparent
contradiction and try to solve it. But if Rainer himself is there, all
contradiction dissolves in his mere presence. If anyone asked
me, What kind of a man is Rilke?—I think I could only answer:
He is not a man, he is an apparition, a being here among us from
other worlds. That he was married and has a child seems to me as
inexplicable as though an archangel had a human destiny, for
although Rainer is in the world, he is personally outside it; he
knows and understands it as none other, but he belongs to it as it
were in a different dimension. "To climb far out of life and grow
far out of time"—that seems to me the meaning of his life. I
have never seen a man who could embrace the smallest and the
greatest things of life with equal love and understanding, for
deep within he is above good and evil, understanding the world
of Dante with the same profundity as the life of a beetle on a
grass-blade; he knows what "insight" means as perhaps no man
before him.

A little story he once told me fully illustrates this quality in
him: ". . . how often when out of doors I have watched some
small beetle trying to do something and failing and trying again
and again. . . . How easily God could help it to climb that
stalk! And it is not at all that God will not, but He knows the
beetle would be startled if He helped it, the beetle would probably
give up and think: I have the strangest feeling, as though I
were no longer a beetle at all. So God takes good care to keep
away from the little creature. But I conjecture that, every
time the beetle begins the ascent afresh, it knows nothing
of its last disappointment and defeat; it has forgotten it all and
stands again before a pristine task, full of curiosity as to what
will happen this time and of the most cheerful enterprise."

Ibsen's *Brand* in the Lessing Theatre. It was an excruciating
evening. After the performance we walked part of the way home.
Rilke was exhausted and, as it were, extinguished; we spoke of
the quite senseless rigidity of that destructive "all or nothing" in
Brand, which can lead only to inward and outward annihilation.
"Un-humility" before fate's highest command, Rainer called it;
always *Tendenz*, never the true grasp of the divinely unforeseen
logic of life, of that life which creates even in destruction. "You

D

see," he said, "Ibsen had spirit, the gift of observation, intelligence, anything you like, even a kind of reverence for life, but the greatest gift he lacked: his heart was not big enough, not willing enough, not charitable enough to accept; it took counsel with frigid reason—and so arose *Tendenz*, opinion, and the most obstinate advocacy of that 'opinion'. But enough!"

An empty taxicab came along the street; Rilke called to the driver. We got in and drove in silence as far as my house. At the garden-gate we bade each other good-night. By the light of the street-lamp I could see that his eyes were happy and peaceful again. "The loveliest thing of this evening was your grey silk dress and the black wrap with the gold stars," he said, and smiled. "A whole heaven of stars was around you and with such a heaven all evil becomes negligible."

Yesterday Rainer was with us in the garden. We took tea out of doors in the sunshine, and he told Frau Delbrück about his youth in Berlin, which then was by no means so terrifyingly vast as it is today. "I lived several—or, it seemed to me, many—years in Schmargendorf in a little cottage called *Waldfrieden* (probably it has long ago ceased to exist among all the stone houses that have since been built there), and there I wrote the *Tales of the Almighty*. In the early mornings I sometimes went barefoot—it was still possible then—to see the deer in the rural and quite deserted Dahlemer Wald."

Exciting plans are discussed, dropped and raised again; they almost disturb the satisfaction of these tranquil days by the uncertainty they bring and the feeling of disappointment their non-realisation might produce. Everything seems to hang in the air. When I look at my still empty trunks I remember that Rainer once wrote me, "You cannot believe how my trunk intimidates me; when I come to think of it, we have had so much to do with each other these last few years that I know all its habits, but it is quite ignorant of mine. A week before I leave, I can see by the look of it what sort of mood it is in and whether it is going to make things difficult for me. I have more dealings with it than with any of the other things that count themselves mine, and yet we have remained as it were on a footing of mutual respect, in which I am the subordinate party. If I were to address it, I should have to use its full title, but we only make signs to each other—I, many small ones, and it, a few large, sweeping signs that elude me."

No, my trunk has no history at all; it is still quite new and, as it were, without fate of any kind. But I believe it will be the first to experience something quite improbably beautiful: *We are going to Paris!*

The thought that the Andersen room will soon be there no longer is very sad. Some strange, indifferent person will live in it, and will have no idea who lived there before. The hours we spent there, the many talks, all the music, will be over and done with; the piano will be taken away. Greatly, infinitely, as I look forward to our journey, I am often overwhelmed by sudden fears when I think of what Rilke wrote of Paris in one of his first letters:

". . . this, to my feeling, desperately outlived and out-suffered place has come to weigh on me so heavily that I could not even show it you with an unburdened mind, beautiful as it is in its unique essence . . ."

Will the old melancholy attack him afresh, the fear of life, of himself, of other people? I have no clear picture of Paris and have never had the wish to go there. Now the simple thought that Rilke lives there has made it wonderful and loveable.

Busoni and Frau Gerda are going there too. He is playing in the Sechiari subscription concert. My dear colleague, Josef T., will be in Paris at the same time on his way through to Switzerland. Perhaps I shall be able to see Rodin at Meudon. Rilke has told me a great deal about him. It lay in the diversity of their natures that he and Rilke, who were such close friends, were compelled to separate; their ways were too different; the path of each "was never that of the other". None the less the parting was infinitely painful to Rilke because it took place amidst mutual misunderstandings. The *grand ami* probably suffered from it also, though he seemed the harder of the two, and was "a great child and a lonely sage". Rilke says that diverse natures are combined in him, crossing and conflicting, and that his art, his genius, can be fully understood only through this polyphony, "which finally booms like a mighty orchestra of God".

Rilke recently told us an amusing story: He and Rodin took long walks together around Meudon and it often happened that

Rodin would suddenly stop in the midst of a conversation and make a note in pencil on his cuff before walking on. On some of their walks this stopping and note-making happened very often, and when they reached home, Rodin's cuffs were generally completely smothered with notes. He would throw them into a corner of his bedroom and put on clean cuffs, which on the following day were covered in their turn with writing, and joined the others. Woe, if Madame Rodin ever attempted to take this towering mound of linen to be laundered. *"Mais, ma chère, que faites-vous? Mon dieu, mes manchettes!"* cried Rodin indignantly. And so they had to lie there, these most singular of "MSS"., till they had been sorted and copied. The first draft of large parts of his book, *Les Cathédrales de la France,* were written down in this way.

Rodin does not know a word of German. He read *Faust* for the first time at the age of sixty, and in a French translation. He knows nothing of Rilke's work except a few translations from *Malte.* Rainer maintains that this absolute one-sidedness, this concentration on his own creative art, is something to be reverenced, for it means complete absorption in his own God-given world, the comprehension and portrayal of that world down to its ultimate roots and up to its highest peaks. He says one reacts to Rodin's creations, especially "The Thinker", which stands in front of the Pantheon, as though it were a revelation of a higher sphere.

The last afternoon in the Andersen room. Tomorrow the piano will be fetched away. Thank heaven all kinds of new plans remain to be settled, and this prevents our melancholy becoming too black. We set out tomorrow. Busonis cannot leave till next week. Now Rainer has suggested that we go first to Munich, then through Innsbruck to Zurich, Berne or Basle, and thence to Paris. I feel afraid of Paris; I know too much of the torments that afflicted him during all those years there. But Rainer has said something so beautiful that I am once more ashamed of my fears. He said:

"I cling to my much maligned room with a new forbearance since *such* letters, the letters to you, were written in it; for, believe me, Benvenuta, they *are* the testament of my whole life, yes, in a sense, of all the rest of life that still awaits me . . ."

With these words I take leave of the Andersen room. The future is uncertain, uncertain the fate it will bring us, but reality is so abundantly rich that it seems to justify any life, whatever it may be, "that still awaits me".

Retrospect

LOOKING back on all that has happened, it seems to me as if those weeks in Berlin were among the happiest in Rilke's life, as if in those tranquil days he was at rest, unburdened by past or future. He lived for the day, for real things; he gave happiness to the few chosen persons with whom he was bound in inner community; he gave it by his presence, by his personality, which drew into vital relationship with him all who were privileged to be near. However much he received of love and gratitude, he was always the giver, the light wonderfully illuminating the inner world of the mind, the most understanding and the kindest of men. In strange contrast with his outward shyness was his inner life, for it was full of sympathy for everything that came from the world and from people, and also—as a true aristocrat in the widest sense—full of aversion for all that was base. It seems impossible that anyone should ever dare to utter a *double-entendre* or tell a smutty story in his presence: the essential loftiness of Rilke's mind would have crushed such an impulse at its inception. To him, as to scarcely another, apply the words of the great poet: "I hate the mob, I demand people." He could speak with touching sympathy of his washerwoman, of an old housekeeper whose husband had met with an accident; he could sit a whole night with a dying tramp in some wretched hospital in a Paris suburb, bringing a last ray of light to the miserable existence of this stepchild of life. But he had to feel humanity, even if it were often only a crushed and wasted humanity. When he felt that, all the bonds of convention and class-distinction disappeared; then it was the human being alone that engaged him, and he felt bound to it in the great community of life.

Rilke went out in search of persons in his own very individual way, just as, when a young poet, he had gone out in search of God. And on his journeys through many parts of the world, wherever he went, he found people: in Sweden, in Egypt, in Russia and in Italy. He "learned" people, explored their "countless variations" and yet remained solitary himself, for he failed to find the echo he sought. He knew people, or believed he knew them, but they did not know him. They accepted his sympathy, his inherent self, as a blessing, just as a sick man accepts the healing early morning air of the mountains, but of his inmost grief they knew nothing. Perhaps this was because he always stood above and outside human relationships, even those in which he seemed to be closely involved; it was not friendship but the spirit of friendship, not consolation but the symbol of consolation, not love but the longing for love.

It is really tragic both for Rilke and the people about him that he could say to me, "I often lost myself in people, gave myself away and got nothing in return—and that is why I admit no one really deeply to myself except you."

And when I objected that he had real friends, he said, "Yes, there are two kinds of friends: the one kind are warm-hearted people who like me on account of my books and come with definite claims which I cannot reject. But my books are telescopes; if you look into them, all kinds of things fly across your field of vision—sky, clouds, objects, apparitions, more authentic than in your normal experience, but those things are not I. You are the only one who knows that. The other kind allow me to make considerable claims on them—a country-house, a park, a mansion, where I could keep house all alone with a staff of confidential servants who count me as one of the family. Every time I accepted one of these great chances, it proved to be something beautiful, but when I left, I felt that somehow I had wasted it, for there was no deep attachment. Once I let it go, it shot away like a branch one pulls down, loaded with fruit, and I was just where I had been before."

I asked whether it did not bring him happiness that he gave so much to his friends by his mere presence or by becoming involved in their affairs, but fundamentally he would not admit it. "So long as their humanity does not concern me, I understand and know it down to its cruellest recesses. And whenever I was under an obligation to it, it crippled me and I could do nothing." Only thus perhaps can one understand why people did not know him, did not *recognise* him, for he "could not disappoint them" and kept his deep inmost being locked up "like the tradesman with his attar of roses".

Again and again, when we were walking in the woods or spending an afternoon in the Andersen room, we talked of all these things, and I came to recognise the dualism that made him seek people and avoid them as soon as he had found them. On one of our last walks by Wannsee—it was a day of unusual warmth and brightness—we sat down on a seat by the water. Rainer had taken off his hat, the spring sun shone on his brown hair, and with head bent he seemed to be listening to the soft plash of the waves. A great bird flapped slowly across the lake, and round about there was a deep stillness. Suddenly he took my hands in his, looked at me with eyes full of deep affection and said, "Did I ever speak to anyone before you were here? No, dear heart, I don't know by what means I communicated myself to you. To speak to you is not to act outwards, but to go within; it is to grow a little where no one sees, as a child stirs in its mother's womb."

Then I took his right hand and put my face in it. My inmost heart was full of unspeakable gratitude, and it must have streamed across into his soul more completely than words could ever have carried it. All the sorrow that was to come was still asleep and far away, only a wishless happiness filled that sacred hour with its imperishable blessing.

Journey

THEO and Betti Delbrück came to the station and brought a fine, well-filled luncheon basket as a parting gift. "Flowers only fade and we thought Herr Rilke would rather have apples and cakes. It's the greetings from mother that make the basket so heavy; they are on the top," said the children. They laughed and talked about our next meeting so that there should be no sadness. Rainer too was fresh and gay. He joked with Betti, asking her to give his kind regards to the windmill and to Presto and Tilli, the two dogs in the neighbours' garden.

As the train drew out of the station, the children's little waving handkerchiefs disappeared, and Berlin was gradually swallowed up in a damp, whitish, morning mist. Then a new world arose. Rilke knew all the towns we passed and told me of his journeys and experiences. Bamberg, Nuremberg appeared and fell behind, wonderful little Gunzenhausen with its ancient houses and city wall, like a picture of Dürer's day. Rain had begun to fall, the air was moist and cool, but we were travelling south towards a warmer spring.

At midday we took lunch in the dining-car, and Rainer was much amused because the waiter addressed him as "Your Excellency". "Perhaps he does it because between the omelette and the roast veal I said something about the German Legation in Copenhagen. Do you think it was that?"

He was as happy as a child. I was not at all surprised when a little girl, who entered our compartment with her mother shortly before we reached Munich, went straight to Rilke and said, "My name's Lotti. What's your name?"

"He is the uncle who knows the Christ-child," I said, "and Snow White and Herr Baum and *den lieben Gott*." Presently the child was sitting on my lap and Rainer was telling her the story of the thimble from his *Tales of the Almighty*. He told her, not word for word but with every detail and a few fresh impro-

51

visations, how the thimble came to be *der liebe Gott*. The child listened enchanted. When he had finished, the mother said, "Many, many thanks, *mein Herr*; you ought really to write that story down. Have you just made it up? You are almost a poet."

"Do you think so?" replied Rilke with a doubtful smile. But the woman reassured him, "Yes, really. You should become an author and write stories for children!"

Then the train entered the great, noisy main station of Munich. The child and her mother disappeared in the bustling crowd with trunk, handbag and two dolls. Porters hurried along the platforms; luggage was unloaded, and we were standing helpless amidst a crowd of laughing, jostling people. Then came salvation in the shape of a hotel porter who, with a "Good evening, *Herr Doktor*", loaded our luggage on to a little truck. We had reached our first destination.

Rainer stayed at the Hotel Marienbad, I with my sister Maria in Nymphenburg. It was a long time since I had seen her, and I wanted to spend as much as possible of these few days in her company. So while we were in Munich, I saw Rainer only twice at Maria's and occasionally when we met in the town to make little purchases for our journey. He was very pleased that I too was fond of looking into shop-windows. He gave me eau-de-Cologne and a beautiful travelling cushion, and was delighted when I could scarcely tear myself away from an enchanting cosmetics shop. "You do not buy soap, you *pluck* it, as other people pluck fruit from a tree," he said wonderingly, as I chose the soap I wanted and had the smooth tablets of delicate mauve, green and bright yellow wrapped in tissue paper and packed in a carton.

Later, in the tea-room at the Hof-Theater we met an old friend, the publisher, Hugo Bruckmann, and sat at one of the charmingly-laid little tables, by the light of yellow-shaded table lamps, drinking delicious tea from thin Chinese cups. Bruckmann, an uncommonly fine and intelligent man, was delighted at meeting Rilke, for whom he had a deep respect. The two men launched into recollections: Rilke talked of Tolstoy, from whom in Russia he first learnt the right way to drink tea. Tolstoy had always prepared the Russian national beverage "with almost solemn rites"; fresh lemons had always to be ready on the table. Bruckmann recalled jokingly that there is always a common factor between opposites, and even Tolstoy and Balzac were at one when it came to the loving preparation of drinks.

"Yes," said Rilke, growing very serious, "somewhere, in some loftiest sphere, what is great of all great men is the same. Only the manner of harbouring what is great within oneself and of shaping it creatively out of oneself, of giving it form, that is so infinitely various, and we can scarcely comprehend it. Tolstoy was fanatical and ruthless, Balzac was superior and stood above events and opinions. Tolstoy needed "evil" or ugliness so that he could battle with it—he was a peasant, or thought he was—Monsieur de Balzac did not need it. Tolstoy made an assault on "evil", Balzac, so to speak, "distributed" it. Monsieur de Balzac, the aristocrat, called one of his creations to him, Vautrin or some other of that innumerable tribe; then he took the evil and served it with two fingers across the table to Vautrin, like a magnanimous creator. Monsieur de Balzac did not need evil; Vautrin needed it and Balzac had it at his disposal. *Voilà*, that was all. The coffee, 'lovingly prepared', poured out its savour and he could go on writing."

The hour with Bruckmann ended our stay in Munich. Next day we continued our journey.

I was glad to see my homeland, the Tyrol, again: Innsbruck, the *Nordkette*, the little castle by the river where my dear grandmother spent her childhood and youth. At that time Rilke did not like the mountains. He said there were such things as "exaggerated landscapes". Glaciers seemed to him monstrous, and he had an almost frightened dislike for Switzerland. "Perhaps some day I shall learn to understand mountains; so far we have had no intercourse with each other," he said—and he was to be proved right.

At Innsbruck it was warm and dusty; the *föhn* blew over the town from the south, making the air heavy and the landscape hard and over-bright. In the morning we took the little electric tram to Hall, to see that lovely old town. But the mountains towered near and menacing above the roofs; the sky shone gentian-blue and the air was close, as though a thunderstorm were coming. We could scarcely breathe.

Rilke suddenly looked so ill and exhausted that I asked him

anxiously whether we ought not to go back to Innsbruck. Yes, he wished to go back, but he would not allow me to accompany him. I was to visit a friend, as I had intended, and call and see him for a moment at his pension before going to my hotel. So he went alone. But I had no peace and was almost glad to find that my friend was away. After a hasty lunch I hurriedly caught the afternoon train.

Rainer was in his room. He lay, dressed, on the divan and I was shocked to the heart: his eyes closed, his face dull grey, his forehead drawn with pain, he looked like a dying man. "*Ah, dieu merci,*" he said in a low voice as I came in, but it sounded more like a groan. I bent over him horrified. He spoke French, which was unusual. "*Ça fait si mal,*" he said, and put his hand over his eyes. No, he did not want a doctor, only something cool on his eyes and forehead. So I sat by him hour after hour, made compresses, changed the wet bandages. They brought me ice and valerian drops, which he liked. Later he let me give him tea and then fell asleep.

Gradually a little colour had come back into his bloodless face. Now he lay there peacefully, relaxed, free from pain. His tranquil face was inexpressibly touching, almost boyish. I put the little lamp on the floor behind the divan, so that the light would not trouble him when he woke. I told the very helpful and friendly housemaid to look in again and listen for the bell or any other noise. She promised that she would telephone me if necessary. Then I went back through the dark, deserted streets to my hotel. I was too anxious about Rainer to sleep. I tried to read, but my eyes constantly turned apprehensively to the little telephone on the bedside table, and I wondered whether it would suddenly begin to ring and bring me some terrible news. Today for the first time I had seen the powers of destruction that threatened Rilke's bodily life. Might they not penetrate into his soul again, bringing back those frightful depressions from which he had suffered so severely and so long?

So the night passed. As day was dawning a thunderstorm broke at last, relaxing the unbearable tension of nature, bringing a long, refreshing rain, clear air, coolness and sleep.

Cold, rainy days followed. Clouds hung low and hid the mountains. Drizzling rain dripped from roofs and trees. It was cold.

Rilke felt well enough to continue our journey. So we left Innsbruck on the morning of the next day but one and took the train across the grey, rainy Tyrol to Switzerland. At the Arlberg the skies brightened and in the afternoon the lake of Zurich lay spread out before us in the sunshine.

Goethe was right when, joyously impatient to see the Eternal City, he raced through Italy, feeling no deep interest in anything but Rome. Mentally we were already in France. So Zurich, Winterthur and Basle were nothing but stations on our route, though the days were beautiful and stimulating: A steamer-trip on the lake, a walk in the mountains, wonderful views of the hinterland, early Böcklins in Basle museum, the Rider at the Cathedral, the view of the Rhine from the terrace of the *Drei Mohren*. But Paris waited in the distance, Paris in spring! Could we help hurrying impatiently towards it?

And finally in Basle we almost missed the train. I was sitting on the terrace of the *Drei Mohren*, waiting for Rilke, who was to come in a car to take me to the station. It grew late; at last he came, rather breathless. When we were sitting in the car he explained that it was all the fault of the soap.

"The soap?"

"Yes. I bought it yesterday in a little shop. I was rather distraught and didn't really notice what they had given me. Then it was lying on my washstand—not very nice, smelling of musk; I couldn't possibly use it. But I couldn't simply throw it away, that would have hurt its feelings too much. So I packed it up nicely again, in green paper, put a little silvery band round it— and hid the whole thing at the back of the window-sill. The chambermaid looked as if *she* would like it—and so we shall both be served."

He told me all this so charmingly and with such delicate humour that I realised at once how much consideration—if one can use the word—even for lifeless objects, was part of his nature. So I could not laugh as he had expected.

But the cream of the joke came when we were standing in our compartment and the servant from Rainer's hotel handed through the window two bags and—a small green package done up with a little silvery band. *"Monsieur a oublié ce petit paquet dans sa chambre; il était auprès du fenêtre,"* he said, proud of his French. He was delighted with the extra tip. Then the train moved out—Rilke had his soap. I am sure he kept it after that, "so as not to hurt its feelings".

Soon we had left Switzerland behind and were travelling deeper and deeper into France. A mild and lovely countryside spread out before us. It was as though the land were under a spell. Between spring-green birches by little watercourses light-grey cattle were grazing. They did not move, but stared wonderingly at the train with big peaceful eyes. Then the spires of a town rose out of the distance; the train sped past them. A child waved from a solitary house at the edge of a wood, and above all the sky, veiled in silver blue, spread a soft light over the scene.

But my impatience flew ahead of the train, spanning the distance, and was not satisfied until, as the sun was setting, we steamed at last into the Gare de l'Est.

We found a big, very dirty and exceptionally ugly station: crowds surging to and fro; people shouting for porters; shrill whistles of departing trains rending the smoky air. Then we were standing in a hideous square outside the station. Vast streets branched off in all directions; everything was noisy and dirty.

The first impression of the city I had longed for with such impatience was so depressing that I felt I should like to get back into a train and go somewhere where it was quiet—to the mountains, the sea, anywhere away from all the noise and bustle, the tall, ugly houses of that multitude of streets that seemed to lose themselves in infinity.

In front of the station were cars, horse-cabs and little omnibuses, and these I loved at first sight. They had six red-plush seats inside, and a small mirror, decorated with fresh flowers, between the little windows. We hired one of these jolly, homey little vehicles; a man who looked like a cheerful gnome skilfully juggled our cases on to the roof, handed us our handbags and umbrellas, and swung himself on to the box beside the driver. The door slammed and the fat, brown horse set off at a comfortable trot. From the Boulevard St. Sébastien we turned past a great triumphal gateway and were soon in a maze of narrow streets. Rue de l'Echignier, Rue Bergère, Rue Feydeau, I read. Everywhere suspicious-looking individuals, young men and girls, were sitting outside the numerous wine-shops, which were open to the street; they were bawling and singing; newsboys were crying the evening papers; in the shops, also still open, fish, meat, bread, brandy, vegetables, old clothes, wigs and boots were being sold.

I must have looked at Rainer with some bewilderment, for he said, with his kind smile: "This will soon be over, then you must look out on both sides . . ."

Our conveyance was already turning out of the Place de la Bourse into the Rue du Louvre, and there it was—the legend— Notre Dame, the Tuileries gardens, the Louvre, the bridges, the river, Paris, like a lovely dream-picture in the frame of the window, subtly dissolving in the blue haze of the falling dusk, unreal and yet as familiar as though one had always known it. Tears came to my eyes; we held each other's hands, and Rainer said: "Yes, this *is* it." Then we drove over the Pont du Carrousel and stopped at the Quai Voltaire.

Rainer, dear and kind, thought of everything. He had reserved me a room. I was to go quickly and wash, and then, if that were possible, come down quickly to dinner. He would wait for me in the dining-room and later on show me his *atelier*, his home.

My room on the second floor was large and furnished so wonderfully and cosily that I had to linger there a while. Above a beautiful old fireplace hung a large mirror in the Louis XVI style; candles were alight in two many-branched candelabra, and on the dark-red carpet in front of the hearth was a great, deep-blue glass bowl, in which anemones were blooming in all imaginable colours. The windows were covered by curtains of a large, flowery pattern and, when I drew them aside, there was the Seine, there was the city, spread out before my eyes. Paris! Paris in spring! ". . . beautiful in its unique essence."

Paris

(*From the Diary*)

PERHAPS the only way to remember times and incidents that seem to one unreal is to cling to their details. Otherwise they would sink deep into the mind, like a dream-image that has faded in broad daylight and melts like early morning mist over a lake.

Berlin was the quiet, happy present; Paris is the uncertain, tremulous future. I still scarcely sense this city; I know nothing of its true nature, but I feel that I could lose myself to it, fall under its spell; other, unknown fates take form in it; it embraces everything—joy and despair, pain and delight.

My little hotel has something uncommonly likeable and homely about it. Rainer says that foreigners hardly ever stay here; the guests are mostly country nobility or good middle-class families from the provinces. Thus I am quickly getting to know a slice of French life.

The house is run by two old ladies, *Madame la propriétaire* and *Mademoiselle sa sœur*, and it has, apart from the concierge, two waiters, a boots and four chambermaids. Monsieur Alphonse in a white jacket and apron told us all this as he served us. To my surprise he gave us oranges and southern fruits before the soup, a common custom in all the Paris restaurants.

Rilke proposed that immediately after dinner we should go to his *atelier*. He was not in the least tired from the journey and so we set out without delay. When we left the hotel it was already dark; a light wind moved the trees on the quay, the lights of the bridges were mirrored in the Seine and, although it was evening, the sky still glowed with the last mild light of the vanishing day.

Rainer said, "You will see: the light is different here from what it is in other countries, not as though it shone on the houses, bridges and gardens, but as though the houses, bridges and gardens, yes, the whole landscape, radiated light from within."

It was, he said, rather a long way to the Rue Campagne première. Should we take the Métro? I wanted to walk and so did he. "It is wonderful, isn't it?" said Rainer, "to walk for the first time in a strange town, to feel oneself walking and taking everything in, as though it had just been created—squares, houses, clumps of trees behind the railings of locked gardens, which one has never known and which yet were always there, as though they had waited for you, like that house, that room, where your letters—those letters so infinitely yours—have long been at home, where my many letters to you were written."

We walked through the streets hand in hand. Sometimes I closed my eyes and let him lead me, and thought: There was a first time in Berlin too, the time I went to him, but then I had never seen him. Now he was walking at my side and his dear, deep voice was speaking to me. Then he stopped, I opened my eyes and saw that we were standing in a little street outside a many-storeyed grey building. Rainer rang the bell. After a time the concierge came, "*Voilà*, Monsieur Rilke!" she cried, delighted to see him again.

With a stump of candle given us by the old woman we lighted our way up the stairs, past many light green doors, almost to the attics. Then Rainer unlocked a door, struck a light, and a very big room, of which one wall was occupied by a vast window, opened before us. With one glance of love and gratitude I took in all those things I knew already from his descriptions: Rodin's writing-table, the little desk where Rainer worked, the books on the shelves, the coat of arms of the Rilke family framed on the wall, the green-shaded lamp on the table, the curtain in front of the big bookcase.

Rilke had put his arm round my shoulder; he led me to the window. The indefinite contours of the cupola of the cathédrale des Invalides soared above black, silent gardens into the darkness; here and there the lights of distant houses could be seen through the branches of trees. It was very quiet; only sometimes the rattle of carts and the hoot of motor-cars came remotely from the great, noisy Boulevard Raspail. Here in the room it was tranquil and lovely, and through the stillness came that beloved comforting voice: "Do you feel how I live now, live in you, live a new life of the mind in the wonderful fact of your coming, safe in you? You will feel, you must not do other than feel, Benvenuta, this pure uprising of my spirit to you, this devotion of my nature, wherever you may be."

Later I walked about the room; I could not help touching the objects as though blessing them: the ink-pot, the brief-case, the desk where he worked, the arm-chair, the little Russian figure of Christ in dull silver. Then I went home. Rainer took me to the street-door. Up in my room I opened the window and saw him wave to me, then his slight figure was lost in the shadows.

It is raining and the air smells of fresh earth. Although it is only ten o'clock there is no one to be seen in the street. On the wet pavements the street-lamps are mirrored and the shadows of the tree-tops swaying in the wind; single stars twinkle through flying cloud; the Seine flows past my windows, its hasty waves gurgling softly. Oh, mysterious city of night and spring! Here in my dear room the bunch of anemones shines on the red carpet. How full of blessings life is; my heart overflows with them.

Good-night, dear, dear Rainer. And thank you!

My first day in Paris is over. It was crammed with pleasant experiences. Delightful it was to wake in the half-dark room with a sense of happiness at being here.

The bronze clock on the mantel-shelf struck six. It plays the "*Air Louis XIII*" three times a day and even keeps correct time. I hurried into the adjoining bathroom and not till I had washed did I go to the window and draw up the blind.

The sun must have just risen. The early morning sky was aglow, and the gleam of its waking light was reflected in the Seine, still dark where its hasty flood passed under the spans of the bridges. How wonderful is Paris in the early morning! The trees are already in tender leaf. The quay is still and empty except for a dealer in vegetables, who pulls his barrow of cauliflowers, lettuce and carrots down the street, calling cheerfully, "*Choufleur, mesdames, de la salade, chou-fleur . . .*" But he has no luck, everyone is still asleep. Across on the opposite bank, the white pleated curtains are almost everywhere still drawn. The booths of the booksellers on the quay still dream of Racine, Lafontaine, Musset, and all the rest of the wonderful contents still locked up inside them. A little fawn dackel comes round the corner, accompanied by a housemaid, who is carrying in her basket two bottles of milk and a large white loaf. Then the street is empty again.

I could not stay in my room. Taking hat and coat, I ran downstairs. Monsieur Alphonse was just coming out of his pantry with a pile of table-napkins. "So early, madame? Would you like coffee? It is ready."

No, all I wanted was a short walk before breakfast, and the good, solicitous Alphonse advised me to put on something warm, for the morning was fresh.

I resisted the temptation to cross the Pont du Carrousel into the Tuileries gardens, which were already bathed in sunshine, for I wanted to see them with Rilke. So I wandered past the hotel through the Rue des St. Pères into the Quartier St. Germain. Here I witnessed a charming little idyll, which could not have happened in any other great city in the world.

Through a narrow side street—I believe the Rue Perronet—came a boy of about ten years with a flock of goats. He was barefoot and carried a little stick in his hand with which he guided his stubborn flock. But the most astonishing thing was the women, who came out of the old houses with buckets and jugs and let the boy milk his goats into them. One girl even dragged two great earthenware jars of fresh milk through a doorway into a grassy courtyard, where an old man with a blue cap on his snow-white head was sitting in the sunshine.

Outside little shops, still closed, stood chattering women. When their turn came, they threw each other a few words of greeting. Everything was peaceful and friendly on this golden morning, and when at last I found my way back to the hotel, happy and very hungry after my long walk, I found that a messenger had arrived from Rilke and a card lay on my table beside a bunch of lovely peach-coloured roses.

"Good morning, dear one. I hope you are well rested. Shall we lunch at one and then go into the town? Please let me have word by the messenger. He is a trustworthy lad and also has the most beautiful summery name that a rose-gardener could wish for: he is called Juin!"

By afternoon the sky had clouded over and it was raining, so we took only a short walk through the Rue de Rivoli and across the wonderful Place de la Concorde to the Madeleine. There we had a magnificent view from the steps down the broad Rue

Royale to the farther bank of the Seine. Standing in the shelter
of the porch between the columns with the broad steps below us,
we looked down at the traffic of this tempestuous city. From all
sides cars dashed past, a flood of pedestrians filled the wide
street. Today it was a throng of moving umbrellas, but despite
the bad weather, I felt a breath of *joie-de-vivre*, an atmosphere of
gaiety, filling the streets and hanging over the whole city.

Well-dressed people sat in the open verandas outside the cafés
engaged in lively conversation. I was struck by the cheerfulness
and happiness of practically all the faces. Waiters in white
jackets carried piled trays and accepted most diverse orders with
an air of extraordinary good humour. It seemed that these
people, often very dissimilar, met in a world of mutual respect
and friendliness.

In the Brasserie Viennoise, near the Opera, we drank delicious
Austrian coffee—I could have wished Busoni with us—and ate
"Indianer mit Schlagobers",[1] which naturally reminded us of our
youth. Rilke told me of birthdays when he was a child and of
favourite cakes; I talked of my first toy, of which I have a vivid
recollection. It was a little brown one-horse carriage with gilded
wheels and a white horse. "Good heavens, don't tell me it had
headlamps! How ardently I used to long for such a toy. But it's
too late now, I suppose," he concluded with a sigh.

Childhood is a magic word for Rilke; he never tires of tracking
down that time "rich in tears and pleasures, like a priceless gift
received, unconsciously possessed and lost before one knew what
it was".

Back in his *atelier* this afternoon, I was shown a little old
faded portrait of his father. "He had the delicately coloured
daguerreotype made hastily for his mother, when, just seventeen,
he volunteered for the Italian campaign in his penultimate year
in the cadet corps."

It was touchingly old-fashioned, and Rainer seems especially
fond of it. "Does it not present the young, handsome face once
for all, as though one saw it with the eyes of his mother, in its
grave, scarcely smiling presentiment of fresh and adventurous
experiences? Once in my childhood I saw it among my father's
papers; later it disappeared for years—it was no good enquiring
about it—then after his death I found it one day among his

---

[1] A kind of éclair with whipped cream.

belongings, framed in this faded old red velvet frame, and I felt, as I recognised it, how unutterably it had knit itself into my heart."

We had more and more stories to tell each other of our first conscious years, and Rilke could not get away from the subject. "Benvenuta, what *was* it then? What was it—that warmth, that wonder, that uninterrupted compulsion to act so and not otherwise, that deep, radiant sense of rising tears? I read in St. Augustine, 'Where could it have gone?' Is childhood still in us, having no place whither it could go away from us? Perhaps it sank too deep into us, and later we turned away to the things of this world—and now here we stand, our faces overflowing with strangeness, and ask, What was it?"

When the evening came we did not wish to go into a restaurant among strangers, where our peaceful and lovely mood might have been shattered, so I fetched all we wanted from a near-by shop. Rilke made tea and I laid the table with fine old cups and plates from his glass-fronted cabinet.

Later Rainer stood at his desk and read aloud his translations of Michelangelo's sonnets. His face, bent and tranquil, with the fine brown hair and the pure line of his profile, stood out against the soft green of the curtain. I do not believe I have ever heard anyone read more beautifully, and I thought I had never heard anything finer than the sonnet to Vittoria Colonna. One forgets completely that the poem was originally written in another language. It is sonorous breath, heavenly harmony.

Rainer accompanied me to the hotel and at the door gave me a little packet "to be opened upstairs". It is Goethe's *Correspondence with a Child*[1] in a fine old leather-bound edition. Inside the cover are the names of those who have owned it, and under his own name Rainer has written mine. How well he knows how to make a gift!

Yesterday with Rilke in the Jardin Luxembourg.

How many of his new poems have been written here! How often has he walked up and down these avenues, sat on one of the seats and watched the children at play, sailing their little boats on the pond. ". . . Oh childhood, shifting comparisons, whither, whither?"

These trees and stretches of turf, these ponds and avenues

[1] *Briefwechsel mit einem Kinde.*

happily combine the impression of nature and of the highest
horticultural art. You would like to think that you played here in
your own childhood, while the grown-ups, students and
graduates, with grave faces and many books, sat smoking or
studying on the benches or walked in earnest talk between the
trees. This is something Paris possesses beyond most other
cities: you feel as though you had been here before, in childhood,
in a dream or in a former existence. Thus you can be happy here,
forgetting that, side by side with the evidence of the greatness of
past generations, stand stony witnesses of bloodiest history.

As we walked from the Luxembourg gardens down the
Boulevard St. Michel to Notre Dame, Rilke told me the story of
the cathedral. The structure was begun in the twelfth century.
It was adorned with statues, pictures and painted windows, each
century adding its contribution, until the so-called classical ideal
mistook and denied the high significance of the Gothic. In the
name of an "ideal" the church was robbed of its ornaments, the
altars were destroyed, most of the statues demolished, and in
1793 the festival of the Goddess of Reason was held in the
desecrated church, which had been declared the *"temple de l'être
suprême"*. Then it became a warehouse for storing flour and
vegetables, and was not restored to the service of God till the
beginning of the nineteenth century.

"Then it seemed no longer a cathedral," said Rilke; "it was a
poor, humiliated, persecuted, downtrodden something; but
none the less these trials had not been able to break its proud
spirit, and the sufferings of so many years make it still more
venerable for us. Must we not love it for the sake of its secret
greatness, that conceals within it the destiny it has survived?"

On entering the wide nave one is struck by the newness of the
interior decoration: there is nothing old except the magnificent
rose-windows over the main doorway, a lovely fourteenth-
century Madonna over the *porte du cloître* and a series of reliefs
on the choir of Jehan de Bouteiller. But the tracery, the façade,
the splendid, bold arches of the buttresses, the king's gallery, the
whole symmetry of the building are intact and unspeakably
beautiful. Rainer says we shall hear high mass there on Sunday.
It is celebrated very austerely, no doubt according to traditions
many centuries old. Mass in Notre Dame is not sung to in-
strumental or organ music as in other churches.

The Busonis, who had announced their coming, have not arrived. We waited for them at Foyot's till three o'clock. Rilke had ordered a wonderful meal. Only in Paris, the city of great contrasts, does one realise the true meaning of the tradition of Brillat-Savarin. The way the famous "crépes" are prepared on little mobile trolleys in the restaurant before the eyes of the guests is in itself delicious. I do not think anyone who has not been here can have any idea of the bewildering magic of Parisian hors d'œuvres. But it turned into a gay luncheon *à deux*, despite the fact that we had expected the Busonis and were disappointed at their non-arrival.

Rainer thought of something to console us for our disappointment. "We will go to Versailles." I asked if we might call on Rodin on the way. I knew that Rilke and he had somehow been reconciled, and that, although they saw each other seldom, an easy, friendly relation had been established between them. But Rodin was neither at his country house nor in Paris.

"Do you know where he is? Somewhere in the south of France staying with Renoir, who is teaching him—to paint! The two old men really go on learning from each other. Of course, Renoir can scarcely hold a brush and has to have it bound to his wrist; but, all the same he still works and gives Rodin lessons, and, in return, Rodin teaches him modelling. Isn't it wonderful, this conquest of the body by the spirit, which still directs these two friends, despite their age, towards new horizons!"

We walked down to the Seine. The boat was already waiting at the quay. Few people went aboard and we sat on the deck in the sun. Then the little steamer moved down-stream, gliding past houses and gardens, suburbs and factories, and was soon in the green countryside. We got out at Meudon and walked across open meadows, by country houses and gardens, up to the "Villa des Brillants". Rodin has described this beautiful country so vividly in his book *The Cathedrals of France* that one could almost imagine one beheld again things long familiar, things that have grown intimate and dear. Here was the countryside around his house, the far view over St. Cloud and Sèvres, the river, the distance lost in shimmering light.

And Rilke is right: the light has a mild heavenly sheen; it changes constantly: now bright, delicate shadows of thin clouds float over the expanse of country and the Seine gleams like silver;

now bright sunlight pours over the spring-green crops in the fields, the bud-decked fruit trees, while the distance is veiled in a blueish haze and children in bright-coloured clothes walk like ambulating flowers down the sunny roads.

But Rodin's house is dreary and uninviting. It looks desolate in the happy landscape. Rilke says that Rodin does not live here in winter. The house is very hard to heat, for the heating system has pipes that open into the rooms and it is so badly contrived that most of the house is draughty and almost uninhabitable.

Rodin has no feminine companion to take care of him, no real friends to grace his home. Rilke says that now he associates with unworthy people who exploit him. "Perhaps you would be able to help him a great deal with your music, but he is never alone; there are always people round him who use him for their own ends. Formerly it was almost symbolic of his way of life that he greeted every guest with '*Avez-vous bien travaillé?*' Now he goes on working only to earn money for these creatures."

I wish we had not gone to Meudon. Rilke's stories, the house itself, the whole impression was so hopeless: human weakness and genius combined in a great creative personality that is growing old in loneliness and unhappiness.

Somehow we were both sad as we reached Versailles, and suddenly I had no more interest in the state chambers of Louis XIV or the famous *galerie des glaces*, but I wished to see the stairway of the orangery. Standing in front of it, I knew that no one had been able to understand and express its spirit and beauty more completely than Rilke in his lines:

> "Alone between the balustrades that bow
> their heads in ancient homage soars the stair:
> slowly and by the grace of God and so
> up towards heaven and out to nowhere".[1]

The park of Versailles is magnificent, especially the *parterre de l'eau* in front of the palace and, in contrast, the wooded area, a spacious green solitude. In great ponds, ancient trees are mirrored, their crowns, bending towards each other, forming Gothic arches. At the ends of avenues of spring-green fresh stretches of water glitter; far views open across meadows and

[1] " . . . *so steigt, allein zwischen den Balustraden,*
die sich verneigen schon seit Anbeginn,
die Treppe : langsam und von Gottes Gnaden
und auf den Himmel zu und nirgends hin. . . ."

pine-edged clearings. The most extreme contrasts—clipped, stiffly laid out hedges, and walls of foliage—form a harmonious whole with untouched nature.

We forgot Rodin's depressing house; we wandered for hours in the mild afternoon sunshine and on our way back saw the two charming little palaces of Trianon with the famous pink marble fountain and beds of tulips in bloom.

Later we took tea in the Trianon Hotel. It is furnished entirely with "king's furniture", heavy old chandeliers, white and gilt chairs upholstered in wine-red brocade, authentic dark-red carpets. Old French oil-paintings and coloured engravings hang on the silk-covered walls. A noiseless, well-trained staff served deep-golden tea with a confusing array of sandwiches and *petits fours*. The long walk had made us gay and hungry; the silver tray was soon emptied of its rich load—to the silent surprise of the waiters and our own amusement.

Rilke can be as merry as a boy. His bright eyes shine then with a childish light. Forgotten are the burdens that so often oppress him; he surrenders to an unconstrained and infectious gaiety. He told a story about Ellen Key and her quarrel with a Danish cab-driver. In the end they would have come to blows if Rilke had not snatched the whip from the cab-driver's hand. "But dear Ellen at once lost her temper with me. She thought it was going too far to try to interfere with a person's—in this case the cabby's—freedom of action. I apologised and said if she really wanted a thrashing I was almost sorry that she had been denied it through my intervention. At that she sided with the cab-driver against me, pressed a tip into his hand, climbed back into the cab and drove off without saying good-bye."

His way of telling this little story made it a thing of inimitable grace and humour. When I remarked that Ellen Key's way of treating her friends did not make her any the more lovable, he said with a smile, "We are, after all, as I once told you, thoroughly dissatisfied with each other's work and human characteristics; none the less, there still remains a sort of memory of the time when—sometimes—we agreed. And that gives us the right to be rude to each other now and then in a friendly way."

The sun had gone down and we had to set out for the station. The way leads down a long, straight road which comes, after a series of gentle undulations, to the Rue de Paris. With its many lighted street-lamps it looked like an arch of stars. Rilke calls it the suspension bridge. Before the train came in we looked at the pictures in the waiting-room—Pau, Orleans, Chartres, splendid churches, lovely old streets. I should like to visit them all!

At home I found a telegram from Frau Busoni: *"Arrivato!"* Monsieur Juin must have been there, for there were moss roses in the blue vase. Their delicate scent was fused with my happiness: the Busonis had arrived! I told Rilke the news as we went down to the dining-room, and we read the programme of Busoni's concert in the *Journal des Débats*.

The Secchiari subscription concert is held at the Palais des Fêtes. A violinist is also to take part. I would rather have heard Busoni alone, but the Parisians like their concerts to have variety. Worse luck! Rilke pointed out that the concerts here, as in London, begin at four in the afternoon. One goes in one's afternoon clothes and the men keep their hats on (a barbarous custom!) In the intervals the audience walks up and down the gallery and corridors.

The days are sunny and warm. Everything is in bloom. Tuberoses, parma violets, mimosa and big, scented, long-stemmed carnations are on sale in the streets. Forget-me-nots shine in round baskets of plaited straw. Pansies and grape-hyacinths are resplendent in rich purple, wallflowers in coppery red and golden yellow. It is a tumult of colour. In the churches the altars are adorned with fresh lilies; girls kneel in devotion before the images of the saints. The Catholic conception seems deeply rooted in the common people of this city, though it is famous for its worldliness and levity.

I have seen a great deal in my walks through Paris: the tower of St. Jacques, the most splendid building of its kind, palaces of the period of the *roi soleil* and the Sainte Chapelle with the famous old glass of its windows. Rilke tells me that the windows in Chartres cathedral are said to be still lovelier, but I can hardly believe there can be anything more wonderful than these. They are separated only by narrow columns. I also admired the pointed arches and traceries above the altar, on the roof and in the choir, and how beautiful is the rose-window, like a more delicate sister of the two rose-windows of Notre Dame! They have survived the storms of war and revolution, an eternal symbol of high culture.

On the way home I got the seats for the concert and met Rilke at my hotel door.

"D'Annunzio will be at Busoni's today," he said; "I don't know whether you would like to meet him?" No, I did not wish to meet strangers in Paris, and Rilke fully understood. But he had something else on his mind: "If a young woman should happen to bow or speak to me—I mean at the concert—please be kind to her."

"Of course. Who is she?"

"Marthe. It's hard to explain to you who Marthe is. You had better see her for yourself. A poor girl, quite young, quite sensitive, very clever, extremely receptive to everything beautiful. I can truly say a pure heart in a despised and depraved profession."

At home we had never spoken of such girls. Our strict upbringing had not even allowed us to guess that they existed. Even when my sister and I were grown-up, we heard only by accident of "fallen women". With our sixteen and eighteen years we did not fully understand what was meant, but it seemed horrifying and aroused a vague sympathy in us.

Now for the first time I heard from Rilke the story of one of these poor creatures, and it was a sad one.

A German lady, Frau Werndl, had interested herself in Marthe and saved her from a house of ill fame. But the girl's blind and unhappy instincts caused her repeatedly to break away from an orderly way of life. "Now she is living with a Russian who beats her," said Rilke. "She is desperate but she cannot leave him. Sometimes she comes to me to borrow books. She looks after the flowers; she loves her little tame birds. I have taken her to museums and given her many good books to read. Her gratitude is childish and touching. You can hardly imagine what potentialities there are in her, what breadth of thought, how much beauty and understanding—but none the less she will never be able to get free. The sinister, the terrible, is too strong in her. I can speak only to you of the life she really leads, for who else would take all her inconsistencies lovingly to their hearts? Even Princess Marie, to whom I have often talked about Marthe, thinks I am in love with her. So I keep her a secret from my nearest friends. Is that right of me?"

"Who is Princess Marie?" I asked. I did not dare to speak of Marthe's fate and of how it troubled me, but Rainer saw it in my eyes, nodded to me affectionately and said thoughtfully, "I mean, you know about all my friends, for you are so deeply in my life that I think there can be hardly anything that you do not know."

And so I learned that Princess Marie was Rilke's motherly friend, that her name was Thurn und Taxis, and that she lived mostly on her estates, sometimes in Bohemia, sometimes at her castle, Duino, on the Adriatic. Duino was a miracle of beauty and peace amidst lovely and noble scenery.

"I should like to take you there some day," said Rilke. "There is the sea and in the White Room the piano on which Liszt has played, and the home and source of the elegies[1]—which I suppose I shall never finish."

His face, his glance, were suddenly as though extinguished, but only for a moment; then he passed his hand over his eyes and asked, "Shall we go now?"

On the way to the concert hall we came to an ancient and very large square. It was the bird-market. Song-birds were for sale in hundreds of cages, large and small. There was such a singing and trilling and fluting and whirring all over the square that we stopped. Rilke seemed bewitched; he did not want to go and we nearly missed the opening of the concert.

The Palais des Fêtes is a very tasteless building. One feels one is entering a covered swimming-bath or a panopticum. The entrances to the hall have curtains instead of doors and in front of them stand gaudily-dressed servants holding lances. As you approach the entrance these "guards" present arms. First you must show your ticket, then the curtain is drawn aside and you are allowed to enter. Rilke had never been there before. He was horrified that Busoni was to play in such a "circus".

The numbers of the seats are attached to the cross-piece at the foot of the chairs, so we had a long search before we could find our places. My astonishment grew: people were walking up and down the gallery smoking cigarettes, the men wearing bowler hats. The audience, mostly very well dressed, seemed to regard the concert as a kind of social function at which music was an additional attraction.

[1] *"Duineser Elegien"*, published in English as *Elegies from the Castle of Duino.*

It was incredible that no one protested against the monstrous bad taste of the platform. The piano and the music-stands for the orchestra stood on a kind of stage; in the background was a garish and badly painted pseudo-Japanese landscape, and on each side a large sign with a painted forefinger indicating the way to the lavatories.

The audience chattered, laughed and shouted greetings to each other in various languages. Many of the faces were exotic—Javanese, Chinese, a few Indian women, gentle and taciturn, in their beautiful national costumes. But so great is the power of personality that the hubbub suddenly subsided only to burst out again as a roar of applause—Busoni had appeared on the platform. All superficial annoyances had vanished.

My beloved Frau Gerda sat near us, and someone next to me pressed my hand. Josef, Busoni's faithful adlatus, the best and most popular pupil in the group to which I myself had once belonged, was sitting beside me and whispered something unintelligible in his pidgin German. Then a wave of happy excitement flowed through the silent, listening crowd. Busoni had begun to play.

Marthe, poor little Marthe, was there. I saw her come up to Rilke in the interval, a beautiful, very childlike face, framed in light brown hair. She was dressed simply but in the best of taste and she bowed to Rilke with the grace of a little princess. When she caught sight of me she made as if to withdraw, but Rilke pushed her gently in my direction. "*C'est Marthe,*" he said, and I held out my hand. Marthe did not take it. She looked at me and her lips trembled. Suddenly she uttered a low sob. "*Ah, chère, chère madame, merci!*" she said, and was gone.

At the end of the concert, Busoni was in the artists' room, surrounded by a crowd of people, "who were quite ready to eat bits of his dress-coat," as Josef said. He was talking to a short, conspicuously ugly man, quite bald except for a few hairs at the temples and round the back of his neck. When he turned I saw his sallow, withered face—a large nose, rather protruding eyes spoilt by the baggy skin beneath them, and a mouth like an actor's, worn with much speaking.

Busoni greeted me and introduced his companion. It was Gabriele d'Annunzio.

My first thought was, How can this man have such power over

women? How is it possible that Duse—— Then, small and almost too elegant, the poet bowed to me and said a few most amiable words—which I forgot immediately afterwards, for Frau Gerda embraced me and whispered the name of the place where we were to meet at noon the following day. It was impossible to exchange two consecutive words without interruption. I was disappointed, and so was Rilke, for he had looked forward so much to spending a pleasant evening with the Busonis. Now they were besieged by strangers, and we, their friends, had to stand by, looking on.

We went back to my room and Rilke read a chapter on music from Proust's *Du côté de chez Swan,* a book he had recently given me and which we had discussed with Busoni in Berlin.

I know of no one who can read as well as Rainer. His voice is soft and has sometimes a slight lilt, especially when he speaks French. It is not true to say that he reads beautifully; it is more than beautiful, it is an intense expression of a higher state of existence. I think Fra Angelico must have read thus, or Meister Eckkart.

An early morning walk in the Tuileries in glorious weather. An old man was seated on an iron garden chair on the *terrace du bord de l'eau.* I could not see how he was dressed, or even whether he wore a coat, for he was covered from head to foot with sparrows, a wave of sparrows engulfed him. When he raised an arm to feed his little friends they remained perched on it, only pressing a little closer towards his hand, while a fresh flock settled at once on every bit of his clothing that had become exposed.

At this early hour the few visitors to the garden practically ignored the old bird-lover. *"Charmeur d'oiseau"* was the name applied to him by an old woman working with hoe and broom between the flower-beds. He was generally here, she said, even in the winter, and no one quite knew how he lived, for he never seemed to eat anything himself, but gave everything to the birds. Sometimes a pigeon flew down from the roof of the *Grand Palais,* but generally he kept open house for sparrows only.

I thought of Rilke's description in *Malte* of the old men feeding the birds: "You could take them for meditative ramblers, those homely-looking men of meagre, in every way unassuming, appearance. But you are mistaken. Do you see that left hand as it feels in the slanting pocket of the old overcoat, finds something small, brings it out, and holds it clumsily and conspicuously in the air? Before a minute has passed, two, three birds are there, sparrows, hopping curiously towards him. And if he manages to satisfy their very exacting sense of immobility, there is no reason why they should not come nearer still. At last one flies up and flutters nervously for a while level with his hand, which (God knows) holds out a little crumb of stale, sweet bread with unassuming, indeed renunciatory, fingers. And the more people gather round, keeping, of course, at a proper distance, the less he has in common with them. He stands there like a candle, burning, shining with the last of its wick, kept quite warm by the flame, and still quite motionless. And how he tempts and entices—that is something those silly little birds can never understand. If there were no spectators and he could stand there long enough, I am certain that an angel would suddenly arrive, overcome its distaste and eat the stale, sweetish crumb out of the worn old hand. But, as always, there are people there to prevent it. They take care that nothing comes but the birds, and they claim that he expects nought else. And what else should it expect, that old, rain-bleached scarecrow, sticking a little sideways in the earth, like the figureheads of ships in the gardens at home? Is its attitude due, like theirs, to having stood, sometime, somewhere, in the forefront of life where the movement is greatest? Is it so faded now because once it was bright?"

How well Rainer knew the sweet, simple habits of strange creatures whom fate and the world had forgotten.

In the afternoon friend Josef called and brought a breath of life into my quiet room. I ought to have a grand piano. "What has happened to Sonata 111?" he scolded. "And the Bach C-major Cantata?"

Josef is very stern when it comes to study. He always supervised our work at Busoni's and gave us good advice. He had picked up a great deal from the Master. When it comes to work he is a genius. He is enthusiastic about Rainer, whom he has never seen except, so to say, from a distance. "Zis Rilke! Splendit man! Got bless him." When the object of his veneration came to tea and chatted with him, Josef was quite enraptured. But all the same he remembered before leaving to make me swear to go next morning to Schneider's, a big piano house, where instruments of all makes and from all countries are to be had on hire.

When Josef had gone, I had to explain to Rilke who he was. I told him that the "adlatus" was of German-Russian origin, was at home in every country in the world, and spoke German, English, Polish, Russian and French all equally badly. He and his parents just managed to escape starvation till he met Busoni. Busoni taught him for nothing, as he does all his pupils, and found him, despite his youth—Josef is only twenty-four—a professorship at Warsaw. An exceptional talent and a loyal lovable person. His idea that I should have a piano here is excellent. I will go to Schneider's tomorrow morning.

This morning at ten o'clock a negro appeared at my door. When he was shown in, he handed me with polite composure a purple envelope, bowed deeply and glided away on noiseless feet. I foresaw something unusual and was not disappointed. "Gabriele d'Annunzio will be happy to see Madame on Thursday next at the Hotel Meurice. *Déjeuner dinatoire*, two-thirty."

No answer was required. I suppose no one ever thinks of refusing an invitation from d'Annunzio.

I did not really want to go, but Busoni, whom we saw at midday, thought it a pity to miss this "*théatre paré*".

"D'Annunzio is half-way between a poseur and a genius," he said. "You will find it stimulating and in many ways bizarre."

The Busonis cannot come because they are returning tomorrow to Berlin, but Rilke has also received an invitation. If he is there I shall be safe from any kind of "*accidente*", so I shall go after all.

The Busonis, Rilke and I lunched at Langer's in the Champs Elysées, and the culinary conversation of the two men was delightful to listen to. Rainer explained solemnly and in detail the procedure for making apple-tea; Busoni talked enthusiastically about *scartozetti* and *scampi*. Poet and musician inspired each other to gastronomic hymns. Rainer's were rather ascetic, but Busoni's had a truly Gallic ardour. At the end of the meal Monsieur Langer charmed us all with a Viennese *Kaiserschmarren*, prepared with his own hands. Then Rainer and I drove to Schneider's, while the Busonis went to the Bois.

Josef is right. Schneider has a wide selection of fine pianos.
I tried about twelve. Rilke can distinguish the finest variations in
the timbre of the different instruments, but unfortunately he still
insists that he is quite unmusical. "I know a song when I have
heard it often, but I am quite incapable of reproducing two
consecutive notes. You must admit that that is proof of
complete lack of ability."

But when I told him that he had a very subtle sense of tone, he
was pleased and gladly accepted my suggestion that he should
have lessons in listening. "But if you find after a time that you
can do nothing with my ignorance of music, then just drop me,
for I'm a donkey!"

The young piano-salesman turned discreetly to me as Rilke
was examining the instrument. *"Excusez, Madame, il n'y a que
trois mois que j'ai commencé à apprendre l'allemand: Monsieur a dit,*
'I am a donkey'. *Qu'est ce que c'est:* donkey?"

I managed to hide my laughter, and told him, *"Monsieur
voulait dire qu'il aime beaucoup la musique; il adore Beethoven et
Debussy."*

"Ah, Debussy!" cried the young man with enthusiasm, and at
once recommended a small, black, semi-grand that stood half
concealed behind the door. *"Americain, mais le ton parfaitement
'scave', comme vous dites en Italie; fait pour exécuter la musique
italienne et française."* Evidently he took me for an Italian, for
when we left, he cried, *"Evviva l'Italia,"* and promised to send
round the Baldwin piano immediately.

Before Busoni left he told us a little incident that is typical of
the spirit of the French people. When he and his wife got into
the cab to drive to the station, he called merrily to the driver,
"À Berlin!" The old man turned gravely and shook his head.
"Pas de souvenirs de la guerre de 1871, Monsieur, s'il vous plaît."

Rilke found it touching that the driver should have responded
in this way to a joke so harmlessly meant. And I think I see his
point.

Now our dear Busonis have gone again. The pleasure of
having them here was all too short-lived and, as usual, we had to
fight for a few brief hours of their company. There were too
many people who "threw themselves at him", as Frau Gerda
says. She assured us laughingly, "I often have to act as a

F

blotting-pad for Ferruccio and absorb much of what they want to say to him. Otherwise he would never have a moment's peace."

The usual Englishwomen had appeared even at the station; the violinist Szigeti was there, a few Russians, looking as wild as Tartars, and our Josef, whose eyes filled with tears as the train drew out of the station. "I am so lonely," he sobbed. "But Josef, you have your wife here," I comforted him. And he cried, still with tears in his eyes but with a beaming smile, "My wife is splendit girl, isn't it?"

What strange things one experiences here! For instance, a Catholic Mass combined with a fashion-show at St. Sulpice, the most worldly church in Paris. Negro priests celebrate High Mass, served by negro ministrants. The expensively dressed children of the elegant "white" worshippers are accompanied by negro servants. There are probably fewer negroes in the German colony of Cameroon than here in the heart of Europe. Is this not a danger for us? No one seems to give it a thought. In the parks, too, black nursemaids are everywhere. They are reputed to be loyal and very docile. Possibly, but I would much rather see children in other keeping.

The luncheon with d'Annunzio is over and it was quite extraordinary. The intentional originality and skill of the décor, the way we were received, our host himself—I could not get rid of the impression that a play was being performed—tirelessly, uninterruptedly and with genius.

Sitting next to me at table was a young diplomat, who is feared for his critical mind and sharp tongue. He whispered to me: "This is the divine Gabriele's day for a pained smile. Don't be surprised if suddenly he says with the happiest expression that he would like to commit suicide."

On d'Annunzio's right was a very beautiful brunette, exotically dressed and wearing magnificent diamond ear-rings. On his left drooped a pale, excessively slim girl, who blushed crimson whenever he spoke to her. She picked nervously at her white lace blouse and seemed ready at any moment to burst into tears, though for no apparent reason. The conversation was in French. D'Annunzio talks brilliantly and is a complete master of the language.

White and black china horses stood as decoration on the huge plate of glass that covered the table instead of a cloth. We drank apéritifs out of smoke-grey glasses of Roman shape and thin as a breath. Before the soup was served our host apologised for having no cook. As deputy he had an Andalusian nun, who had fled from a convent in Madrid and taken refuge with him. The advantage was that she practised faith-healing on the food so that there was never the smallest error in the menu.

No one could guess whether he himself believed it or not. This extraordinary man is a master of the most various rôles. He blushes like a boy, laughs like a child, speaks in the hoarse tones of an aged and dying man, or flares up like an ecstatic youth. If his appearance were as perfect as his literary style, one could better understand why he is adored by all these women. But as it is, aging, withered, complacent, he makes a melancholy impression and looks like a caricature of himself.

After luncheon, Turkish coffee, iced water and verbena-blossom tea were served in the studio, and d'Annunzio showed his guests the antique casket containing his famous collection of perfumes. The most precious are a flagon of genuine attar of Roses which belonged to Lucretia Borgia and Macchiavelli's bottle of smelling-salts.

The ladies present almost swooned with admiration. I looked at Rilke, who seemed to have turned himself into his own shadow, and was almost submerged in one of the big chairs. Only the bright eyes were alive in his immobile face, watching, half humorously, half sadly, the activity around him.

I told d'Annunzio that his *Sogno d'un mattino di primavera*—a book I had read as a girl of fifteen—was still in my opinion the most wonderful piece of writing in Italian, and that I wished its verbal music could some day be presented to German readers in a perfect translation. He replied that all translation is botchery, but the feeling with which a growing child had admitted the *Sogno* "to her flower-fresh heart" was an imperishable blessing, which a poet must preserve on the secret altar of his soul— "*come una fiamma benedetta*," he cried suddenly in Italian.

I do not know whether he intoxicated himself with his own words or whether he really felt a kind of satisfaction or pleasure at what I had said. The impression he made on me was still ambiguous.

How different, how genuine and fine was the evening that

followed. At home Rilke read aloud to me from his *New Poems*. There was much I did not know—"The Inside of the Rose", "The Panther", "The Roundabouts", "Venice", "The Roman Fountains"[1] . . .

What is all the pomp, the power of language in d'Annunzio's verses, splendid as they are, beside the pure world of Rilke's poetry? Ought we not to wish that none but the pure in heart should understand Rilke?

He wants to read with me a novel by his dead friend, Gernard Oukama Knoop, a posthumous work of that extraordinary man, entitled *The A and the O*. Rilke said that before he died, Knoop left a wife and children. He went on to tell me the awesome story of his death. When he was very ill and knew that the end was near, he shut himself off from his family, allowed only the male nurse to enter his room and refused all nourishment. After some days, his wife, in despair, sent to ask whether she could see him, and he allowed her to come in, sent the nurse away and said with a transfigured face, shining with a light of other-worldly happiness, "I have been talking with God and now I can take leave of you."

During the few days that still remained to him he comforted and blessed his wife and children and died at last in their arms, fully conscious and at peace.

Early this morning alone in the Louvre. I saw the Gioconda, which had mysteriously vanished and had reappeared as mysteriously. I remembered that d'Annunzio told a guest recently that the spirit of the Gioconda had come to him and wished to stay, but as that was impracticable the picture would appear again in the Louvre.

One of the women asked, "With or without its spirit?" But Gabriele passed charitably over her naïvety with an indulgent smile.

Now the Gioconda is back again in its old place, but scarcely recognisable through the fine double wire mesh that protects it. I saw a wonderful picture of St. Francis by Giotto, Leonardo's "St. Ann with two others", a Madonna against a gold background by Cimabue, a Millet, Delacroix' portrait of Chopin—

---

[1] *Das Roseninnere, der Panther, das Karroussell, Venedig, die römischen Fontänen.*

Chopin must have looked just like that!—Corot, Manet . . .
The mass of pictures is bewildering. How many times one
would have to go there to get even a fleeting impression of all its
glories!

At home I was welcomed by a whole garden of flowers,
blossoming sprays and roses, roses. Rainer had been there and I
had missed him, but he was to come back in the afternoon for the
first "listening lesson". I arranged my little garden for our
"concert", and *Madame la propriétaire* had to send up her finest
vases.

The Baldwin really sounds very good, different from the
Ibach in the Andersen room, richer, fuller. The bass notes have
an organ tone.

Every afternoon or evening I play a short programme for
Rilke. He listens with great pleasure and understanding. If I
look at him while playing a piece he has never heard before, his
face is full of the most concentrated attention. It is as if light and
shade were passing across his brow; his big expressive lips,
slightly overhung by his moustache, are almost painfully com-
pressed; all his frail figure, as he leans back in the arm-chair, seems
to be listening.

But if it is a melody he knows, the tension is relaxed; he seems
to be at rest. Sometimes when he is utterly immersed in sound
and harmony, he seems to me to be the listening world-soul
itself, and so strong is the influence of his unique personality that
the whole room appears to radiate music.

I have never had so many fresh ideas for improvisation as
when Rainer is listening, and if he says afterwards, for instance,
"May I hear again the phrase before the pause?"—it is almost
always a new turn, an emphasis, that had struck him, and one
that I owed to him entirely. Such inspiration is a wonderful
experience. If I speak to him about it, with pleasure and
thankfulness, he smiles incredulously, and says, "It's all you."
But that is quite untrue.

He is especially fond of Händel, of the *wohl temperiertes
Klavier*, and of Beethoven, though he knows little of Beethoven
as yet. How right Josef is to urge me to study the C-Minor
Sonata.

Yesterday I played Brahms' two rhapsodies, but Rilke did not take to them. "This music seems to me partly empty and partly overladen," he said. "And Brahms' face, as I sometimes see it in pictures, is as alien to me as his music."

Now we are studying together Mozart's Requiem. I have a score copied by my grandfather and I showed it to Rainer, who is very much interested in old-fashioned handwritings. He admired its clearness and the beautiful writing of the text. I played the whole work to him. We are to hear it soon at a concert by the famous *Schola cantorum*.

I feel somehow uneasy because Rilke is not working. He, who values solitude and seclusion more than all else, regarding them as his highest duty and service, is now living entirely in music and in plans for travel. Perhaps it is good for him to rest for once without worrying, without thinking of the strain and loneliness of new creative work. All the same I am sometimes depressed and apprehensive. He wrote in one of his letters, "Work has a kind of primeval and sacred claim on me." Are my presence, my happiness, my deep gratitude, robbing him of something?

When we first considered meeting here in Paris, he wrote to me, "There is nothing to stop you coming very soon, for, apart from me, here is Paris—that is the main thing—and it is quite certain that Paris is incomparably more beautiful in spring than in autumn. . . . I will tell you quite candidly what my attitude would be and it is dictated by obedience to my solitary soul. First, I should take your hand in my two hands, and there it would stay as long as it pleased; but then I should withdraw at once into my normal seclusion, do nothing and give very little. Still, we should have an occasional afternoon, an evening, a walk together, things we have never been granted before and which therefore, in their fewness and rareness, would still be a great deal—and we should have an incalculable number of good things to say to each other." No, he has forgotten his normal seclusion. We do almost everything together. He never thinks of spending less than several hours here daily. Again and again the torment-ing thought comes back to me, Am I robbing his work?

Perhaps it is simply that in these last trying years I have grown used to endless agitations and conflicts, and have therefore come to mistrust the kindliness of fate, the permanence of the beautiful, lovable things that surround me, so that I fear they cannot last but will change into something quite different. How these thoughts torment me! And I must hide them from the one person to whom I can speak with complete freedom, lest he too should be distressed.

The concert in the *Schola cantorum* was a painful disappointment. The old-fashioned hall in the Quartier Latin, Rue du vieux Colombier, seemed a worthy setting for Pergolese's *Stabat Mater* and Beethoven's *Elegischer Gesang*. Mozart's Requiem was to be given at the end. But instead of the choir and orchestra, a famous combination here in Paris, giving a perfect performance, they provided something little short of catastrophic.

Wind and strings were out of tune, and the singers, male and female, laughed and whispered during the orchestral passages. It was as though soubrettes and bad musicians were attempting vainly and with bored indifference to render a requiem mass. We went out after the kyrie. Rilke was quite upset and said that such performances ought not to be allowed. "Where is the least sign of reverence for the greatest?" he asked. "Do you know where it is? Sometimes in places where no one would look for it, unless he knew that a ray of the great light still survives in many a humble and despised man or woman. . . . Marthe came to see me this morning. She laughed and wept. '*Quel bonheur, quel bonheur!*' she cried over and over again. '*Une dame m'a donné sa main!*' And when I asked her why she had not taken your hand, the child looked at me with the tears running down her face, and said, 'One must be reverent,' and ran away. Later, I found on the table a little note in her handwriting: '*Que le Saint Sauveur vous benisse, âme pure et douce.*' It is for you. I have kept it for you."

"Why must so much humility, love and tenderness be condemned to such a degraded existence?" I cried, with emotion. "Why does no one know the answer to all the malice and cruelty of life?" Rilke looked gravely in front of him and said nothing. But on our way home, he told me, as if to answer all these unsolved questions of our human state, the story of the three old men.

"Three old monks lived on the seashore. They were so wise and holy that every day a little miracle was performed for their benefit. Every morning, when they had finished their devotions and went to bathe, they hung their habits in the wind. And the habits stayed there, floating in the wind, till the old men came back to fetch them.

"One day, as they were refreshing their bodies in the waves, they saw a great white-tailed eagle flying over the sea. Suddenly it came down on the water and, when it rose again, it held a fish struggling in its beak. One of the monks cried, 'Evil bird!' At that his habit fell out of the wind on to the ground, and lay there.

"The second monk cried, 'Poor little fish!' And his habit too fell down and lay on the ground.

"The third monk looked after the bird, as it flew off with the fish in its beak, and watched it grow smaller and smaller and finally disappear in the morning light. The monk said nothing— but *his* habit remained hanging in the wind."

"Rainer, is that the answer?" I asked.

"Yes," he said softly. "Don't you think the seer in this Indian legend gives us an answer to *all* the questions we cannot answer ourselves?"

"Dear Rainer, dear Fra Angelico," I said in a voice as soft as his and with deep inward emotion. Then suddenly he drew my arm into his and led me across the street. From a deserted, dimly-lighted by-way several suspicious-looking youths came towards us, and shouted some indecency. They vanished as quickly as they had come, and next moment two policemen appeared, walking in the middle of the road at a safe distance from the house-fronts. Rilke said they did so in order to avoid being attacked.

So our beautiful evening walk was abruptly ended, and Rilke said, quite excitedly, "Promise me that you will never go out alone in the evening. To think of you unprotected in the dark in a place like this—you will not do it, will you?"

But there was already the familiar Quai Voltaire, there were the lights, the bridges, the river, the brightly illuminated entrance to the hotel.

And, as we parted, Rilke said, "Look! The many, many stars! May the whole starry heavens watch over you always and protect you!"

We have been to two very different church services—High Mass at Notre Dame and Mass at the little Armenian Church, St. Julien le Pauvre. Rilke says that the believers in the same religion speak to God through an infinite variety of rites, and all mean the same thing.

In Notre Dame High Mass is of puritan simplicity. Somehow it seems as if this church still feels the ignominy inflicted on it in the cruel past and has never quite recovered from it. The venerable old statues are gone; the church has been robbed of its interior adornments; the walls and arches, blackened with so much incense, no longer exhale an atmosphere of simple devotion and the fervent prayers of centuries; they still seem filled with horror, the memories of a yelling horde of criminals, mad with destruction, who stole or destroyed the precious vessels and ancient vestments. And as though the cathedral can never recover the safe warmth and piety of peaceful times, the rites of its services are rather an austere sin-offering than a humble and loving service to God.

High Mass lasts over two hours. In a monotonous sequence the priests at the altar and the alumni in front of the presbytery intone the words of the Mass. Choir boys in red and white cloaks with their choir-master, a young abbé, stand grouped in a semicircle behind the alumni, and answer the priests with sung responses.

The organ is silent. Only short intermezzi of the simplest kind, rather like preludes, are used to connect the different parts of the Mass.

The service is cool and severe, without that atmosphere of devotion with which the Mass normally binds together all believers.

We sat in the middle of the gallery, where we could see the whole interior of the church. The people kneeling in the pews beneath us were mostly dressed in dark clothes and carried prayer-books and rosaries. We looked down on rows of bent heads. Only a blind man in an invalid chair, accompanied by an attendant, had raised his face, as though his sightless eyes sought a gleam from the radiant colours of the rose-window.

Rilke was sitting in a shaft of light from the blue and red panes. It dazzled him. He was restless, and whispered to me, "If you have no objection we will go over to the Armenian church. The singing there is beautiful."

Coming out of the cathedral door, we saw a strange spectacle. Orleanists and Bonapartists, side by side with representatives of the extreme Left, were loudly recommending their propaganda pamphlets to worshippers leaving the church. Strangers were pounced on by all three parties. But they behaved quite peaceably towards each other, and many a worshipper went off in surprise and some resentment with a whole bundle of assorted philosophies under his arm.

Another world was waiting for us in the little church on the farther bank of the Seine. This early Gothic building, where the Armenians hold Mass, is situated in a very narrow street. An icon, painted with faded pictures on a gold background, divides the nave into two halves. The altar is half-hidden at the farther end. The white-robed priest, who had a long black beard, stood in the sunshine among clouds of incense in front of the entrance and near the icon. His face was turned to the worshippers and he was chanting the Gospel of St. John in Armenian.

Women with handkerchiefs over their heads, postmen, street-cleaners and fruit-sellers filled the pews, which were few in number. Little cheery Juin, our rose-gardener, was there. All seemed to know each other, and everyone seemed to know Rilke, for several children smiled at him and moved aside to make room. Two old women, whom I recognised as the bird-lovers in *Malte*, nodded in a friendly way and shook hands with him as we passed them to enter the pew.

"Fra Angelico among the poor," I thought. Then the voices of the choir swelled out and filled the church.

Notre Dame with all its frozen splendour melted away before the potency of the music that streamed heavenward from this poor little church. It was as though waves of consolation, grace and light flowed from the splendid voices of the invisible singers, from the organ tones of the basses and the pure glory of the tenors. The voices rose fervently into the sunlit clouds of incense. Some of the congregation were quietly crying. But Rainer, completely immersed in the music, had in his eyes an expression of sadness and devotion that moved me deeply.

Afterwards, in my room, he told me that suddenly he had realised afresh the tragic quality of great music.

"For me it is not pain but fulfilment," I answered. But he stuck to his point. "I have felt it today repeatedly—when music speaks, it speaks to God and not to us. The finished work of art has no relationship to men, except that it stands above them. It is true that music has different laws from those of other arts, but if we stand in its way it goes right through us."

"Haven't you often felt that it exerts its influence upon us in the most hidden flow of the blood?" I asked.

"It is like the air of the mountains," he answered. "We breathe it into our spiritual lungs, but who knows how far beyond us it goes and what it carries through us that we cannot apprehend. How it alarms us! And then we stand alone, overwhelmed, and cannot reach to its eternal flight."

He had spoken with great excitement, as though in fever. His bright eyes looked dark; he shivered, though the warm, late-afternoon sun was shining into the room.

When he had sat down, silent and exhausted, in his usual place in the chair by the window, I opened the piano and played a little old song. We called it "The Italian Shepherd", and Rilke was very fond of it.

"Again," he begged, and I played it a second and a third time. When I stopped I saw that he had fallen asleep. The pallor and brownish hue of his face, his closed eyes, reminded me suddenly of the terrible hours in Innsbruck. Again I scarcely dared breathe lest I should wake him. Had it come back, that frightful thing?

Evening came, lights flared up in the street; the dim reflection from the ceiling lay on his immobile face, bent sideways and downward; his left hand, hanging loose over the arm of the chair, shone pale through the dusk. I bent over him; he opened his eyes with a pitiful look of suffering.

"Just think," he said, as though speaking straight out of a dream, "I was in a little, lonely station, deep inside Russia, waiting for a train. But it did not come. Dusk fell, and at last I asked a little old man with a red face and white hair, who looked into the waiting-room, when the train would come. But the old man smiled knowingly and without compassion, and said, 'No train will ever come here again.' Then I got up and went out. The little station was desolate, the broken windows hung down from their hinges. Thick green grass, flowers and bushes were growing between the long-since rusted rails. I had been left behind, forgotten, in that infinite loneliness. And the old man had vanished."

Suddenly Rainer said—and his eyes were bright with fever,

his voice quite hoarse as though with the fear of death—
"Benvenuta, do not leave me alone."

I bent down and laid my hands on his forehead. "Rainer
dear, don't speak. I will look after you. It will soon pass. I will
watch with you till it's gone."

"Oh, your hands—cool, kind," he whispered. Then he sat
still and let me put a wet cloth over his eyes.

What else I said in my deep anxiety to calm him, I do not
know. But suddenly he seemed really to wake up, and his voice
was normal. "Forgive me. I frightened you. I'm better now.
I will go home. No, my dear child, don't worry. I'm all right
again." And he was gone.

(From a letter to my sister Maria.)

". . . I am sure it is wrong of me, but I am writing you today
just as my troubled, overflowing heart dictates. Your letter was
so full of joyful news about your home and your little boy, and
the picture of Mario is so sweet that I could kiss it. And now
comes this letter, full of turmoil and alarm, bursting in on the
peace and happiness of your life. But I think of those ever dear
words you spoke to me when I said good-bye to you on your
wedding-day two years ago—'Never forget that we must keep
close together when times are hard.' My hard times have come—
and I have turned to you!

"You know Rilke. Even if you have seen him only once or
twice, you know who he is and how much he can mean to me.
You have understood it all and been so sincerely pleased with our
deep, and certainly extraordinary, friendship. You have never
asked how it will end. And I, Maria, have not asked that question
either, and perhaps that was wrong of me. I have never asked, I
have been happy with him in the present. Happy because of his
noble and lofty spirit, happy because of his inexhaustible kindness. Every time I saw him was a gift of God to me. And I
thought that if some day he had to withdraw and be quite alone
with his work, then I should be alone again, somewhere in the
world—far away from him, not hearing from him any more but
guarding his holy quietude in my heart. I should almost forbid
myself even to think of him—and if I were allowed to see him
again, I should be happy.

"But it has come quite, quite otherwise.

"Rainer has asked me whether I—whether we should not stay together all our lives. He used a word he normally suspects and avoids, the word 'always', and he said it with such confidence, with such faith and fervour, that I was overwhelmed. I think I turned deathly pale, for all the blood had streamed to my heart.

"He took my hands and kissed them with a movement so heart-stirring and yet reverent that the tears rose to my eyes.

"Then he asked me not to say anything, not one word, in reply: I was to promise nothing, I was only to do what 'from all eternity' I had to do. But he wanted me to know that he prayed to God daily that he might so love me that his love would be a blessing. But if I felt, now or in time to come, that a life like his was too much for me to bear and share, then I was to go back to my own life, 'simply and courageously', without any promises and without thinking of him. But 'from the very beginning of all things we have moved towards each other—that is my faith and my most sacred hope,' he said.

"Dear Maria, perhaps you will never, never understand why my whole mind is so distraught, but now all at once I had to ask myself this: Do I love him as a woman loves a man, as the sole person to whom she is to belong all her life? Do I love him so much that I want to be the mother of his children?

"And I have to answer, No. For me he is the voice of God, the immortal soul, Fra Angelico, all that is superhumanly good, lofty and sacred, but not a human person! I have an unspeakable fear of 'humanising' my deepest and most exclusive feelings towards him, of dragging them down into the every-day, earthly sphere, where they could only exist by completely denying themselves. And, strangely enough, there is something else: somewhere in the world are a woman and a child who belong to him. Do you think one can simply break in upon the rights of these two persons and usurp them? I know they are only external, and that Rilke has long since freed himself from any inward claims. None the less it seems to me that the rights of others—who are not to blame for the rupture that has taken place—must be respected, though I know from my own bitter experience how much suffering and misunderstanding can result from a marriage contracted when one is too young and immature.

"Dear Maria, how you suffered for me and with me in those

three years before the divorce! Such thoughts now break into my own life. Where is guilt, where is clarity? How defenceless one is against the fate decreed for one! Can I tell him all this? No!

"If we had a mother, like that splendid mother to whom Rilke has raised an imperishable monument in *Malte,* how easily everything would be solved and put right in her ever-watchful heart. Then one could kneel before her and put one's head in her lap and say, 'Help me.'

"But, as it is, one is alone again, faced with life-long decisions.

"And then there is something else that I cannot understand: Rilke has taught me afresh to affirm life; he has made life joyous; he gives it all the wealth of his inexhaustible mind, of his inexhaustible goodness; he enriches my understanding of all things, of the smallest and most insignificant of the beauties of nature and of humanity. He has given a great stimulus to my music—and yet he is often the great sufferer, quite helpless, unable to bear the life to which he has taught me to say Yes. Sometimes I should like to help him with all the strength that he has given back to me, to help him even as one takes a child in one's arms, and says, Be quiet—all is well.

"Where is the solution to all these puzzling contradictions? The inner voice answers his question with an imperious and inexorable No. But is that the final answer? Whenever we fail to obey the inner voice, we go astray.

"But have *I* the right to think of myself and my doubts, when *Rainer* utters the word 'always'?"

Before I could make up my mind whether to send this letter or not, I got word from the South Tyrol that my sister's son, little Mario, was ill with scarlet fever. My brother-in-law wrote that Maria had been nursing the child and had now contracted the disease herself. They were both in hospital at Bolzano; the little boy was almost well again, but my sister was dangerously ill. No one was allowed to see her, otherwise I would have gone straight to her.

I can never explain in words how Rilke helped me to bear those agonising days of anxiety, uncertainty and fear for my sister's life; how his loving sympathy and faith in the brighter aspects of our fate helped me to live through those times. He was my refuge, my peace, the answer to every troubled question-

ing. He tried to lead my thoughts toward the great and beautiful, and thus we spent many of those spring days in the open air,
in the country. And there, as we walked through the woods, he
told me of the lives and fates of great men, of Michelangelo,
Vittoria Colonna, Manet and Cézanne. One aspect of the life of
that extraordinary man and great painter has remained clearly in
my mind. Rilke told me that Cézanne often painted out of doors,
under trees, on the banks of streams, and sometimes left a
finished picture lying in a cornfield, forgot it in sketching out a
new idea, and went home. Reapers and peasant women sometimes found these pictures, took them back to the village and
gave them to their children to play with. And in this way many
of his works were lost.

Rilke spoke much of the world and what it vouchsafes and
denies us, of the eccentricities of little men and the strange ways
of great men, and his nature frequently showed itself at its purest
in the countryside, which he loves so much. We often walked up
steep, mossy paths, past little springs, to the ancient monastery
wall in the wood at Meudon, or we sat on a bench in the beautiful
park of St. Cloud. When it rained or when for some reason we
could not go into the country, we would go to the Louvre, where
he taught me to see and understand pictures of different periods,
or we stayed at home and he showed me his few little treasures.
"Really I don't care about possessing things, but there are a few
that cling to me because they do not know where else to go," he
said, as though in apology. Now it was a round, milk-white
pearl, now a faded picture of his grandfather, or "*maman's*" very
old Venetian lace, or a valuable copy of Mistral's *Mireio*, with
the French and Provençal on opposite pages, printed on lovely
creamy paper and bound in grey leather, lustrous as silk. I
admired it, and he gave it me. And we always waited together for
the daily telegram from the hospital. The days were full of
anxiety, till at last, at last, the news came that Maria was out of
danger.

We did not speak of our own lives or of the future. But often
during lonely evenings spent at home reading or writing, I asked
myself: Is it not only natural for a man and woman who are
mentally so close together to spend their daily, outward life
together too? Would it not add to what was already great and
good, would it not make me incomparably happy to be there to

brighten his hours of misery and suffering, to solve his bewildering problems, to be in very truth *benvenuta*?

Once he had written to me: "Tell me, is the universe so old that we can know so illimitably much about each other, as it were from the immemorial across this bridge of sudden existence to the irrealisable? Dear heart, up to yesterday, up to a few weeks ago, I was walking to and fro by a monstrous river; I had been doing so for years, and knew no way of crossing it. For by his own strength alone no one has ever swum across. So I waited, sitting on the stony verge, unable even to see the further shore. And it roared past in its immeasurable breadth, and absorbed me utterly into its roar. . . . It even swallowed up my last store of silence. And I ran and called for the ferryman; I thought he must hear me, but the night-wind drowned my cry, an owl shattered it with its flight, everything denied it. . . . But now this miraculous arch is there in the dawn, and my way leads straight toward it, like a little path through a garden."

Such was the trust that had come to me from an overflowing heart! And was he not himself the consoling voice of my bitterest hours, joyous peace, a present blessing? Could I still conceive of life without him?

Then came the other voice, hard and unsparing, and said, "What do you really want? Do you want to make a human being of Fra Angelico, to turn him into a creature of earth for the sake of your so-called super-earthly feelings. Can't you see what has happened to his work? Can't you see that he lives only through you and for you, that he is blind to everything but you, that he is losing himself in his love for you? Don't you see that one day, if you should dare to subject his life to your influence, to intrude on his ancient right to solitude, he would hate you? Is that not betraying a great trust?

No, cried my heart despairingly, Rainer will never hate me. But the voice was still there and went on speaking: What have you done for him?—You have crippled him, chained him to love. Do you ever think of those words, written for him?—"The way from talent to greatness is through sacrifice".

Do you not know your urgent duty? Dare you stay?

When such thoughts oppressed me, I often got up in the middle of the night and stood in the cool air at the open window and watched the moon shining on the water of the Seine; or with hot, wakeful eyes I watched the rain beating on the window-panes in the first grey blurr of dawn, while the sun and its cheerful rays were still afar off.

At such times I read Rilke's early letters again and again, as though I might find in them an answer to the desperate turmoil of my heart. He spoke of how much he loved "insight", "getting on the track" of things, trying to fathom them. ". . . to look at a dog, for instance, to immerse oneself in a dog, precisely at the spot whence it becomes dog. . . . If I told you where was my feeling for the world, my earthly happiness, I must confess that it was often in the brief, deep, timeless moments of this divine insight. . . . You see, if one loved, that would be the first thing that would be lost—the dog came, an unutterable pain arose because one had no longer the freedom to give oneself up to immersion in the dog. There was someone in the background, who called one 'mine'. . . . And the dog would first have to apply to that person and get permission for one to immerse onself in it for one, imperceptible, secret moment. . . . No dog would ever think of it—or, if it did, nothing would come of it. For if anyone knew, and gave permission so and so many times ('just this once'), that would be enough to make the magical moment for ever impossible."

Rainer asked me if I thought that quite silly and childish. No, I understood it only too well, and I understood that here perhaps was the reason why he left home, because he was not allowed to "immerse himself in the dog"; or if he had once succeeded in doing so, he would immediately have had to describe what it was like. But his understanding of his mother was deep enough for him to know the pain and misery it inflicted on her. To her, the dog was not much more respectable than some waterfront tavern. "How could she understand that her nice-minded son was fond of going there, and not at all fond of being with her?"

All this was at the same time light-hearted, wise and serious. But it seemed to me decisive that the woman who stayed behind would have to be a kind of "sailor's wife", and could have no conception of the dangers and vicissitudes from which one day— or perhaps in the middle of the night—her lover would return, sinister, taciturn, his senses packed with alien impressions, full of alien emotion, incapable for weeks of speaking of it; yes, as though filled with alienated blood.

G

And, a prey to doubts, Rilke would not be able to help asking his inmost self: Is it thinkable that she, who has waited for me, absorbed in her peaceful daily duties, can hide from me her fears, cares, reproaches, the smallest tear of disappointment?—that she can simply be there, like the house, bright by day and indescribably still by night, like the garden, like the humble window on the staircase, like one of the loyal, accustomed, tranquil objects in the house? . . . "If it were love, the infinitely unconcerned, ever present (and therefore unexacting) love, then such a return would be indescribable, like a blissful death, like resurrection. But, I tell you, it is unthinkable."

Yes, I thought, that is true: it is unthinkable. And it was as though the blood of my Spanish forebears spoke to me, the blood of that proud line, the first subjects and companions of Charles VI, whom he took with him on his return to German Austria to reside at the court of Vienna. "No," said those long-dead voices, speaking in spirit to me, a woman of their blood. "No, it is not possible."

But the other, too, the poet, Fra Angelico, said the same, and in speaking understood—Fra Angelico, who knew all the suffering of mankind. And this knowledge came to him because such a thing was beyond the strength of woman, the warm, nourishing, earthy strength of woman, and also beyond the tempestuous strength of man. And he cried aloud out of his tormented heart that if one foresaw, even in the most secret nook of the soul, what it meant, the self-violation, the sacrifice that would be constantly exacted, ". . . Benvenuta, do you not think it would convulse him till he was destroyed by it?"

Why the torment? Why tear it open like a wound that can never heal? And I read, ". . . and if in some superhuman way it were hidden from him and made easy, if he were talked into it, and if he compelled himself with superhuman effort to believe that it is just 'nature'—this thing that can only be achieved by a continuous miracle of God—would not the least that could happen be this: that he would never again find the strength to say farewell!"

Never again find the strength to say farewell! That was it. Rilke would take away from a woman everything she might still have found for her salvation. Why then the superhuman sacrifice? And I went on reading, in defiance, revolt and pain,

". . . if only he had a huge crystal in his garden and could sit there and see the world become distorted and recede, as before he had seen the real world change and grow small. Oh, and his lovely danger out yonder yearned for him and another went in his place, and she loved the other. And he was a corpse in his garden and in his house and the unutterable love around him was suddenly like the love one bears to the dead. For when a man knows his joy and will remain in it, then his joy dies, and he is like a fly in amber, nothing but a dead little dark spot in the beautiful yellow of his dead joy. . . . For, if it is not to happen thus, if he is to go, if the beloved is to *bid* him go, when the caravel is ready to sail—Benvenuta, what heroes they would both have to be! The toughest heroes! Do you see?—I have just realised it for the first time: To speak of love is to speak of hardness."

Was the man who could think out such things as this the same who split up feelings and the good, safe things of life into endless doubts and scruples, errors and negations, and who yet could say, full of overflowing emotion, "Dear, dear heart, it is long since I prayed to God, but now I entreat Him to make me love you with all the roots of my being, so that my love be a benefit to you, so that it buttress your gaiety in you, so that it be the garden at the wondrous season of the year, which you bring surging towards me, immortal joy . . ."

Years later I realised that that night something died in me, and it was not reborn for a very long time: the power of the heart to trust in the immutable, to believe without reservation.

My sister was far away and scarcely convalescent. I could not burden her with my wretched thoughts. I could not reach Frau Gerda, who was somewhere in America with Busoni. I was alone. Only my diary, my silent friend, can tell of that time:

Rilke is ill again. The terrible and painful nervous attacks often last half the day. None the less, he went out today and, when he came back towards noon, he brought me a manuscript, The Seven Poems of the Unknown.[1] He read them aloud, but at first I thought they were by someone else; there is an alien tone in them that does not belong to him. He must have guessed my thoughts, for suddenly he said, "They are no good, are they?" I told him he had probably written them when he was not calm and ready enough. But I immediately regretted those

[1] *Die sieben Gedichte des Unbekannten.*

words, for I remembered that, "a man is lost for the greatest if he produces anything below the level of his present greatest".

And Rilke was already saying, "Do you think that I can ever be 'ready' again? Isn't that all over?"

His face burned with fever and suddenly grew pale again. His forehead, usually so smooth, was contorted with pain.

I took my courage in both hands. "Rainer," I said, "I think I am taking up too much of your time. I am sure you wish to be alone again and work. I too must do more work. Think, I have ten concerts this summer—at Wiesbaden, Nauheim, Kissingen, Blankenberghe, and God knows where else. . . . We ought to be more industrious," I added, trying to speak lightly.

"All right," he said, doubtfully. "The first thing is not to see each other or speak to each other for four days." He tried to be cheerful, but without success, and seemed willing to agree to anything.

We went out together, but Rilke returned home and I lunched out alone. Later, in my room, I took up the score of a piano concerto, meaning to read it through and make notes on the orchestral passages, but I could not work. I saw Rilke's face, his poor, suffering face, and suddenly such an acute fear seized me that I sprang to my feet without stopping to think, picked up hat and coat and ran downstairs. Someone spoke to me and held out a letter but I ran on. In the street I took a taxi and drove to the Rue Campagne première. The long Boulevard Raspail seemed endless; at last we reached the Métro station, the car turned into the little street and stopped at Rilke's house. I did not walk, I almost flew up the many stairs and rapped the prearranged signal on his door. Rainer opened it at once. "Benvenuta, dear beloved child, did you know that I was calling, calling, calling you? . . . Are you really here? Is this not too much for you? Do you forgive me?"

He poured out a stream of feverish questions. Then as we sat in the warm spring air by the open window and I held his hand, he grew calm. He said he was sure he would soon be well again. Princess Marie had invited him to come to Duino in May. She had written to me too and sent me the same invitation; she was eagerly looking forward to our visit. Later, we might all go on to Venice together. Would I like it? Like it! I was touched by the great kindness of the princess, and fired by the wonderful prospect of seeing Duino. Rilke fetched some photographs from one of his many portfolios: a fairy castle of rare beauty, set on a crag; a tower that dated back to the Romans, soaring high above the sea. Another picture: on the main façade a great terrace that seemed to hang in the air and was like a pergola completely smothered in roses; far below, extending over the rocks, a garden with holm-oaks, laurel bushes and flowers. Here was a reality that imagination could hardly have fancied, and we were to be allowed to enter this magic world!

That evening I found the letter from Princess Marie awaiting me at my hotel. It was the letter I had ignored as I ran out that afternoon. She wrote that she was looking forward to having some music. I should feel at home in Duino, she said, among a small party of exceptional people.

She must be extremely kind. Perhaps the visit will clarify much that is now vague and confused. And Rainer! Rainer will surely be able to work again in the deep quietude of a spacious countryside, shielded by the infinite freedom of the sky and the sea. Perhaps all will come right. Only go on hoping, lovingly and patiently.

The days appear to be kind and peaceful again. But Rilke is not working, his good resolutions are forgotten. He is almost always with me, even when I am studying. Then he sits quite still. I often wonder how he can bear to listen to all those runs and repetitions. It seems that now he cannot live without music. He loves our little evening sessions, especially Händel and things by the old masters, Scarlatti, Couperin, Frescobaldi. Sometimes he wants me to go on and on, and then I play for hours. Sometimes we read together: Francis Jammes—some of whose *Prayers* Rilke had translated—that mournful seeker after God, Charles Franck, and a new novel by André Gide, *Les Caves du Vatican*. Gide writes a very difficult French and sometimes, I think, is intentionally scurrilous.

But the best is always when Rilke speaks freely from memory. He has told me various things he remembered from his Spanish diary. Some were so beautiful that I begged him to repeat them. Then I sat opposite him with my exercise-book and wrote them down:

"The almond-trees in bloom; all that
we can achieve here is to recognise
ourselves completely in earthly phenomena".[1]

And:

"Endlessly I marvel at you, you blessed ones; your bearing,
how you wear your giddy ornament in the manner of the eternal.
"Ah, if we knew how to bloom: our hearts would be beyond
all feeble dangers and in the great danger consoled".[2]

And the finest:

"The little birds in the holm-oaks, speaking prose no longer,
versify a little. The heart of one plashed like shallow water.
Whence the ardour of created things? . . . By the brook I
picked marsh marigolds, almost green, a little yellow, quite
fresh, painted into the cup at the last moment. Inside, around
the stamens, an oil-soaked circle, as though they had pilfered
butter. Green odour from the tube-like stems. Then to find the
scent left behind on one's hand, closely related through it.
Friendly girls, long ago in childhood, with their hot hands. . . .
Was it this that so moved one?"[3]

No one else can give as Rilke gives, for who else knows the
perfect way of giving? Indeed, who can give at all? I remember
in my childhood the painful moments when I had to say "Thank
you". When we were given a present, the pleasure had already
fled because an uncle or an aunt, already "touched" in advance,
stood waiting for the thanks of the lucky recipient. It was better
at Christmas, provided the Christ-child or Father Christmas was
the giver, for they were splendidly indifferent to thanks, since

---

[1] *"Die Mandelbäume in Blüte, alles, was wir hier leisten können,*
    ist, sich ohne Rest erkennen in der irdischen Erscheinung".

[2] *"Unendlich staun ich euch an, ihr Seligen, euer Benehmen, wie ihr die*
schwindliche Zier traget in ewigem Sinn.
    "Ach, wer's verstünde zu blühen: dem wär das Herz über alle schwachen Gefahren
hinaus und in der grossen getrost".

[3] *"Die kleinen Vögel in den Steineichen, nicht mehr Prosa redend, dichten*
schon ein wenig. Wie ein leichtes Wasser plätcherte dem einen das Herz. Woher
die Innigkeit der Kreatur? . . . Am Bach Sumpfdotterblumen gepflückt, fast
grün, ein wenig ganz neues Gelb im letzten Augenblick in den Kelch hineingemalt.
Im Inneren, um die Staubgefässe herum, ölgetrankter Kreis, als hätten sie Butter
genascht. Grüner Geruch aus den schlauchigen Stengeln. Ihn dann in der Hand
zurückgeblieben finden, recht durch ihn verwandt. Freundinnen, einst in der
Kindheit, mit ihren heissen Händen. . . . war es dies, was einen so rührte? . . ."

they were not even present. But best of all was when the only real person among those around me, my dear old Uncle Hugo, who unconsciously understood our childish oddities, came from town to visit us in summer at our country place. Scarcely had he arrived, when we would find on our little chest-of-drawers or on the nursery table some of those coloured pencils in which we took such delight. Blue, green and violet paper with a sort of silvery sheen was gummed around them, and in the midst was the finest of all, the "gold" pencil.

Rainer has had similar experiences and understood them completely. He knew too that when grown-ups tried to give pleasure to children, they often gave it only to themselves. How many of those early memories we have in common! He took note of my description of a dear old custom observed in my grand-parents' house. Every Easter Sunday there was a family break-fast. A little lamb of white sugar was placed in the middle of the table with brightly-painted eggs and spring flowers around it. There were boiled ham, fine white bread and different kinds of cakes, and each guest was given a little present, a chocolate hare or an egg.

I never expected to enjoy one of those childhood Easters far from home. But on Easter Sunday morning, Monsieur Juin appeared, carrying a large object wrapped in white tissue-paper. When I had undone the coloured silk ribbons, I thought I must be dreaming of long ago. There, in a shallow basket of bast, surrounded by cowslips, violets and white anemones, was the sugar lamb; it even held a little red pennon, exactly like the lamb I had taken such good care of at home. Under the flowers were little flat cakes and Easter eggs in all colours. And there too were the shining, dark chocolate hares with a delicate scent of vanilla, which had enthralled us as children. How gentle, how touchingly sweet of him, to think of it!

Rainer found me still sitting before his present, quite lost in its contemplation. He was refreshed by a night's sleep and how glad he was to have given me so much pleasure! He had thought of a wonderful plan. We would take the little steamer to Sèvres. "Duino is getting nearer—and you still have so much to see here," he said.

Duino! Will it bring the longed-for answer to all our questions?

My diary, silent, patient friend, how am I to tell you what has happened?

Rilke no longer wishes to go to Duino. He feels again so ill and wretched that he would like to shut himself up, to "creep away like a beast dully dying". There is an inconsolable despair in him. I have never seen him like this before. He says it is all over with his work, he is finished, will never be able to write again, everything is lost. He says he must flee the light of day, escape from the few people whom he loves, in order to "spare" them, to let them forget his failure, his unworthiness. I must have talked to him for hours, I think. I told him of the gifts God had given him, of how many people loved and respected him and were grateful to him, of all those to whom he had brought light and a nobler view of life. I told him that his sole duty was to do everything to sustain himself for his work.

And when, with a gesture of weariness and dejection, he asked me "Why?" a desperate anger took possession of me. I told him he would be neglecting his duty if he did not rid himself of everything that impeded his life and work—if necessary, the Princess, Duino and myself. If he retired into seclusion, it must be a fruitful and creative seclusion, nothing else was worthy of his vocation. I felt I had to wrestle with the evil forces that governed him and, though I was afraid he would be angry, I said all that my heart dictated.

I sat on a little chair in front of him. He was in an arm-chair. My arms were on his knees and I looked up at him beseechingly. I could hardly distinguish his features in the semi-darkness. Suddenly he leaned down and said in a tone of indescribable feeling, "Benvenuta, dear, dear heart, are you not in truth my virginal mother, my child, my dear, dear girl—you with your golden armour, on which everything false and base must splinter? Cannot you see that the flaw is after all irreparable, even when your healing hand touches me? You symbol of all happy life!" Then he took my face in his poor, hot, trembling hands—and we cried bitterly in each other's arms.

For several days I have hardly slept. The weather is stormy. Perhaps Rainer will grow calmer when the moon is past the full. I have not seen him for two days and do not know what I ought to do. I have asked the concierge who looks after him to summon

me if he is ill. For the first time I stopped at the door of his
house without going up!

Rainer came this morning just after breakfast. He asked me to
go into the country with him, to Chantilly, and stay until the late
afternoon. He looked ill but was calm. As we descended the
stairs, he said, with the pathetic shadow of a smile in his eyes, "If
you like, we could leave a week today. We could take the night
express through Geneva, Milan and Venice to Monfalcone. The
princess would send a car to the station. She telegraphed me this
morning."

I was suddenly relieved, as though all those bitter hours had
never been, and I felt that Rilke too was glad to have made his
decision. We smiled at each other in silent agreement. When
we were in the train, he said, with a sigh, "It's going to be a fine
day."

In truth the spring sky covered the blooming earth in full
splendour. We left the train at Orry and went on foot through
the beautiful woods. The dew lay on the young grass; the
meadows were thick with flowers. In a round bed before the
little chateau of "Reine Blanche" the lilac was in bloom.

Rilke drew in the delicious air in deep breaths. He had taken
off his hat and raised his face with closed eyes towards the fresh
wind and the sun. "Do you hear the leaves rustling?" he asked.
"The sound is different in spring from what it is in summer when
the foliage is fully developed and sways in the wind, or in
autumn when the tired leaves, prescient of winter, have to fight
the storms for their transcient life. But now! How blissfully
they rustle, as though it would go on for ever."

We walked on along narrow paths. The sunshine shimmered
on a floor of bright-green moss. A jay swung in the twigs of a
tall beech, and in the distance a cuckoo called.

As we went slowly on, looking and listening, Rilke told me
the history of the wood and of "Silvie", about whom, long since
dead, he had once wished to write.

"She loved a poet named Théophile de Viau, who, after
various warnings, was condemned for his over-free verses. But
they could not find him, because the Duchess of Montmorency
kept him well hidden in her little hunting lodge in the heart of the
wood, waiting for the time when she could help him to escape

under safe escort. A poem he wrote to her in homage and gratitude names her '*la belle Silvie*'. The common people have known her by that name since her death nearly three hundred years ago, and so the wood is called '*bois de Silvie*'. Many of these old trees must have been witnesses of that tender and dangerous passion."

This lovely day ended with a visit to the Musée Condé in the Chateau of Chantilly. Rilke showed me many splendid pictures and art treasures, particularly the unequalled miniatures of Fouquet from a prayer-book of the early fifteenth century. They took the book from its case for him, and we were able to examine it at leisure. The shining colours, the blues and reds of the apparel of the saints, had lost nothing of their brightness; it was as though they were still fresh and moist. Delicate flower-garlands and arabesques adorned the gothic pages and the bold sweep of the initials at the beginning of each prayer. And Rainer spun a chaplet of legends round these darkened, yellowish parchment pages, which many hands must have touched as they paused at a prayer or a picture. Kings and princesses, happy, tyrannical, sad, loving men and women, whose names are no longer known, had owned, loved, preserved or forgotten this book.

Rilke also showed me a unique collection of forty or fifty pictures, hung in a little round hall, from which one had a delightful view of the park. Many of them were very small; few much larger than twice the palm of one's hand. All were framed in narrow strips of bright gilt and all represented the same subject—a single human eye. Eyes blue and dark, brown and grey, stared back at me. They were painted with masterly skill as though on transparent glass, and they made on me an eerie, almost ghostly impression, unique, fascinating and bewitching —beautiful as most of them were. Wise, sad, beautiful, timid, cunning, malicious, laughing or kindly eyes, they seemed together to present the history of all human qualities. And by the art of their creator they seemed to look straight at the beholder, wherever he stood. He was, as it were, completely exposed to them, and they seemed to be trying to fathom all his secret thoughts.

Absorbed and astonished, I forgot to ask the name of the painter. Perhaps even Rainer does not know it, for sometimes he loves to contemplate a work of art without inquiring about its origin or period.

On later visits to Paris I have tried several times to find that room again, but have never succeeded. It is not mentioned in any history of art, not even in the guide to the Condé museum. This made it seem all the more mysterious, and for some reason beyond my comprehension I did not care to inquire about it. I often had unique experiences with Rilke: I never again discovered the bird-market through which we passed on our way to Busoni's concert, and Princess Taxis told me of a similar incident that happened to her with Rilke in Venice.

Perhaps many things that happened to me with him were to remain unique and unparalleled.

(From the Diary.)

Chopin's grave at Père Lachaise is a very popular place of pilgrimage. This largest of Paris cemeteries was laid out at the beginning of the nineteenth century on a site where once stood the house and magnificent park of Louis XIV's father confessor —Père François d'Aix de Lachaise. Almost fifty years later Chopin was buried there. The simple grave with an unpretentious stone, which bears Chopin's face in relief, could easily be overlooked, were it not covered at all seasons of the year with flowering plants, wreaths, shrubs, bouquets and fresh sprays of green. Near-by is the gorgeous monument of Cherubini, so large that it can be picked out from a distance. But it is completely neglected; not a flower blooms in that thicket of weeds; the iron chains on both sides are thick with rust, the once beautiful wrought-iron lantern is broken. Cherubini has been forgotten while thousands make pilgrimage to the grave of Chopin. A charming custom has been preserved through the years: every visitor who places flowers on the grave leaves his card with them. Here are the names of people of all classes, from artisans to princes of Orleans or Ligne, from errand boys to famous musicians, from washerwomen to fashionable ladies.

When Rainer and I came to place a wreath on Chopin's grave, we took half the white narcissi and big, blue and gold pansies and placed them by tacit consent on Cherubini's splendid but forgotten resting-place. Then Rilke tore a page from his pocket-book, wrote on it the initials of our two names and fastened it on with part of the twine that bound the flowers.

Looking back from a distance, we could still see our white narcissi shining on Cherubini's lonely and neglected grave.

Our last days in Paris passed quickly. When it came to leaving I felt I had seen hardly anything. I had been about a good deal with Josef and his wife before they left, for they often came to see me. These two cheerful, happy young people lived their life with gaiety and confidence, though it was outwardly often far from smooth. Then they too were gone and I began to take leave of Paris as one takes leave of someone whom one never expects to see again. The glittering city showed herself in all her magic, in her most shining beauty. Houses and balconies everywhere, in the big squares and the smallest alleys, were being decorated to welcome the King of England.

The place had a festive air. There was practically nothing to be seen of open or concealed hostility to Germany. Rilke and I usually spoke German even in the street without provoking any objection. It was years since one could have done so in Prague. But I repeatedly noticed that there were cards in the better shops and stores announcing that English, Russian, Greek, Rumanian, even Turkish and Arabic were spoken there, but the German language was never mentioned.

On our last day Rilke and I revisited Notre Dame. It was late afternoon and the church was deserted, but there was a light in the organ gallery, and of a sudden someone began to play:

First it changed into a canon and then into the interlaced passages of a fugue for five voices with full accompaniment. The mighty edifice, as though awakened to dignified life, quivered to the might of the music. And we sat together lost in a dream, as in the old, bright, happy days, listening, until at last the voices were silent and the light above the organ went out.

Rainer said he had never heard the organ of Notre Dame before. I suggested that Johann Sebastian's great spirit had come to redeem the cathedral with his music, and he smiled and said, "He alone would have the power and the glory to do so."

That evening I played to Rainer for the last time on the Baldwin piano, but he was silent and depressed and I did not play long. Next morning I packed, paid my bill and saw to a number of things connected with my departure. But I found time to spend a few moments in the Musée Cluny and to look again at my beloved *Dame à la Licorne*; I also visited the Sainte Chapelle, the Luxembourg gardens and the Pantheon with its frieze by Puvis de Chavanne, illustrating the life of St. Genevieve, patron saint of Paris. Finally, before the trunks were fetched, I played to myself on the fine piano that had been our intimate friend for so many weeks. I played the "Italian Shepherd", and wrote inside the lid, "Never forget that you have made music for Rainer Maria Rilke."

Then I took leave of my dear room. How desolate it looked! There was the arm-chair by the window, but Rainer would not sit in it again, reading or talking or listening to music. In the blue bowl before the fireplace were a few fading yellow irises: no one had found time to give them fresh water. The table, where good books and manuscripts had lain, was bare. Trunks and bags were everywhere. It was as if the dear, cosy room had lost its soul—Rainer was no longer there.

Always the same sequence: departure, fresh beginning, completion and again beginning—infinitely! Where had I once read "Nature wants unceasing change, but man longs for permanence!"?

In the midst of these depressing thoughts came that good, considerate old lady, *Madame la propriétaire*, to say good-bye. Then the porter arrived to fetch my trunks, and finally the taxi. Driving along in the open car, I was able to say good-bye to many a spot I had come to love—the Quai Voltaire, the Seine, the Pont Neuf, the Tuileries and, in the distance, Notre Dame—a big star hung in the evening sky exactly over the main doorway. Then the impression of this beloved city was swallowed up in a confusion of noisy suburban streets and the turmoil of the station.

The Rome express was waiting. After some search I found my sleeper in the third coach, where my hand-luggage was already safely installed. I ordered a bottle of *eau d'Evian* from the *conducteur* and settled down.

The train pulled out. For a time I could still see the lights of Paris, then only a great rich glow hung over the place where she must have been. At a curve in the track even this disappeared in the darkness. The train sped on into the night towards the far-away and the unknown.

Duino

I WANTED a cup of tea and a bite of food and, on entering the dining-car, I found Rilke writing at a little table by the window. "I didn't see Marthe again," he said. "I must send her a few lines." I added a greeting and signed it. I had kept the note she had sent me, but I should never see again that charming, unhappy child, destined to end in misery and despair.

Rilke and I soon parted, having agreed to meet for breakfast at nine o'clock next morning. But he told me to look out of the window if I woke early, for the views along the shore of Lake Geneva were exceptionally beautiful.

The gentle, lulling rhythm of the sleeping-car soon sent me to sleep, but I was awakened early by the loud voices of several passengers passing down the corridor. We must have stopped in Montreux: the train was gradually picking up speed, and when I opened the window we were moving fast, and I could see the snowy peak of the Rochers de Naye shining above the waves of Lake Geneva as they purled in the morning wind. I caught sight of two fishing boats putting out from a little harbour, the sails gilded by the first sunrays, of the sleeping town of Lausanne, of a wide, shining expanse of water as far as the French shore with the little bathing resort of St. Gingolphe. Then everything was gone; new mountains, new landscapes spread out before me in the light of the ascending sun.

It was a wonderful journey across frontiers, past lakes and mountain ranges that flashed by as in dream-flight. Breakfast with little table-lamps in the brightly-lighted dining-car, as the train raced for a full half-hour through the Simplon tunnel, then Lake Maggiore, its banks dotted with cheerful villas and magical gardens. Blossoming camellias, rhododendrons taller than a man! For the first time I saw the delicate miracle of mimosas growing out of doors, many still bearing their scented, bright yellow, feathery umbels. Bright pink rose-bowers and lilac-coloured

clematis drooped over stone balustrades, till they almost touched
the deep-blue waters washing round little landing-stages, gate-
ways and boat-houses. The Borromean Islands gleamed across
the water like the Elysian fields, Isola Madre and Isola Bella
were decked with shining, blossoming gardens and overshadowed
by pines, cypresses and deciduous trees.

Then the mountains fell away and the broad, fertile plain
spread out, covered with fields of young maize, bowers of vine,
yellow-blooming pumpkins, fruit trees and olive-groves. And
then, like a mirage, Milan cathedral, visible far away in the
glittering midday sun!

We had to alight and take the train for Trieste, for the express
went on to Florence and Rome, and so we used the hours of
waiting to get a meal and take a short walk through the town. But
it was hot and dusty; Milan showed herself in a most unfavour-
able light.

The Trieste train, coming from Turin, was crowded, but we
found in the last coach a half-compartment which contained only
one passenger, a girl holding in her hand a little book bound in
green and white: it was the *Cornet*.

"Another incident with an unrecognised poet," I thought.
Rilke had already noticed the *Insel*-volume and smilingly signed
to me not to betray him. The girl, immersed in the book, took no
notice of us until Rilke began to speak of the Rotonda near
Vicenza, which we should be able to see from the train in about
half an hour. Then the girl looked up and asked shyly whether
one was allowed to visit this famous building; she was prepared
to break her journey and alight at Vicenza in order to do so.
Rilke explained that the owner, a Countess Valmarana, of
Venice, generally spent a few weeks there in spring and autumn
with her daughter; but in any case, even if the family were not
there at the moment, he would give her a note for the curator,
who was quite well known to him. The girl thanked him
politely and went back immediately to the "Legend of Love and
Death",[1] quite unaware that the author of the book was sitting
beside her.

When the train stopped at Vicenza, Rilke gave her his card
with the promised words of introduction. She looked at it and
flushed crimson.

[1] *Weise von Liebe und Tod.*

"Herr Rilke," she stammered in deep embarrassment. "And I—I didn't—I beg your pardon."

She just managed to get out as the train restarted. Rilke handed out her bag and the book, which in her confusion she had left behind on the seat, and the embarrassed girl stood on the platform, waving to the departing train. I think she was crying.

All we saw of Venice was the station, for by this time it was dark; but as we crossed the lagoon by the long railway embankment to Mestre, we saw the lights of the town and the far-off, winking red beacon, where the great lagoons lead to the open sea. A short journey and we came to our destination, the little, ill-lighted station of Monfalcone. Outside, the car from Duino was standing with "*un carro per i bagagli*" as an old servant called it, while he helped the chauffeur to carry our trunks.

It had begun to rain; the hood of the car was up, and we drove through a long avenue into the darkness. First I made out a small town with a church high up among trees, then the rain beat against the window and everything was lost behind veils of water.

"Piero will be disappointed," said Rilke, pointing to the servant sitting beside the chauffeur. "He is always happy to be able to explain things to guests when they come here for the first time. He is particularly fond of the rock with the Castell Vecchio and tells strangers, who are allowed to visit the castle one day a week, that Dante sat among its masonry with a 'golden pencil' in his hand and wrote with it in a big book his '*canzoni antiche*'. The liberties he takes with the centuries only make his explanations more legendary. Everyone at Duino is fond of the old man. He has served the family for over forty years."

The car drove between high, ivy-covered walls, through what looked like the gate of a fortress, entered the inner court of the castle and stopped at the great door.

A grey-haired lady of middle height was standing in the hall. She had bright, expressive eyes under dark, strongly-marked brows, and a smiling, intelligent face. Her hair was done in little ringlets over her forehead. She was wearing a white evening gown with a short train and copper-coloured silk shoes, and she really looked like one of those Renaissance princesses who patronised the arts and harboured poets, musicians and painters of all nations, allowing them to live for their art and the good of their own souls in surroundings of freedom and beauty.

H

Born a Venetian, she spoke fluent German with an Austrian accent that reminded me of home. Her natural kindliness and ease of manner were precisely as Rilke had described them. Soon we were sitting down to a late supper in the dining-room, Rilke was talking of our journey, and I was able to examine the large and very comfortable apartment. One wall consisted of three enormous windows; several folding-doors led to other rooms; the walls and furniture were dark, and on the richly-decked table were wax candles in tall, embossed candelabra; dark red felt, on which lay beautiful and costly carpets, covered the whole floor. While the table was brightly lighted by the many candles, the rest of the room was in a warm, glowing dusk; I could only make out a few large oil-paintings on the walls, a coloured flower-piece and a landscape over the long sideboard, on which were silver pheasants and partridges.

As we rose from the table, the princess took me by the hand and said, "You look tired. Tomorrow we will have a longer talk. The barometer has gone up; it will be a lovely day and you shall get to know our Duino. There is no electric light in this nest on the cliff, so Annina will light you to your room with a candle."

She kissed me on the forehead and I followed the waiting Annina, who led me through dark corridors to the upper floor, where she unlocked one of the many doors. I almost thought I was back again in my beloved room in Paris. It was a large room with old furniture, flowered cretonne curtains at the windows, a big four-poster bed, arm-chairs and a small chaise-longue, called Balzac. Only the piano was missing, and instead of a fireplace there was a huge, white-tiled stove in one corner, which somehow made me feel very safe. But for the stove I might have thought that a magic spell had suddenly transported me back to the Quai Voltaire.

Two tall paraffin lamps of pink china with rose-coloured silk shades took the place of electric lights, spreading a bright, yet soft illumination. One was on the round table, on which lay also a few finely-bound books, the other on a chest.

I had surrendered the keys of my trunks in the hall; my underclothes and frocks were already unpacked and neatly arranged in the wardrobes. Even my little tortoise-shell paper-knife and the red leather note-book Rainer had given me in Paris were lying beside the blotter, pen and pencil on the writing-table.

In the adjoining cabinet two great jugs of hot water were standing ready, wrapped in flannel, and next to them a bottle of choice lavender water. Everything was cosy and had the indescribable old-fashioned comfort of old houses, where one can live graciously without central heating or desk-telephone, as though afar from the hurrying everyday world.

I tried to look out of the window but could distinguish nothing in the darkness. It was still raining and from somewhere far below I could hear the roar of the sea and the beat of waves on the cliff.

But the miracle of that night was the choir of bird-voices. Hundreds of nightingales were singing beneath the windows in the bushes of an invisible garden. And above, the castle soared high into the cloudy sky whence came the heavy rain.

In this mighty symphony of great landscape and restless sea I fell asleep.

I dreamed that Rilke had written a sonnet about the nightingales. He came up to me with a happy smile and said, "I am saved. Do you hear the note of the flute?" Then he read it aloud and, as he did so, two brown birds alighted on his shoulder and looked into the book.

I thought, That is not Rainer at all; that is Francis of Assisi who preached to the birds. But d'Annunzio, who sat near-by in a cloak of gentian-blue silk, said mockingly, "*None si deve far pazzo, venite, fratello!*"

"*Dio ha proibito la fuga, rimanete!*" I cried aloud, and awoke at the sound of my own voice. The room was full of light. Outside, the sea was deep blue with a thousand golden sun-flecks on the waves. The nightingales were silent, but everywhere little birds were flitting in and out of the dense bushes, which covered cliffs falling sheer to the water. Sweet scents came in through the window with the morning breeze, suggesting the proximity of heliotrope or jasmine. Everything was ashine, the sea, the near and distant bays, the horizon, which merged with the waves in a golden haze.

After breakfast I ran down into a magic garden of little narrow paths among anemones, tulips and wallflowers. Wild, dark hyacinths grew in clumps and, whichever way I looked, the sea gleamed through the blackish-green foliage of the holm-oaks.

I sat down on a seat among the laurel-bushes. I was close

above the water, and beside me was the old, half-crumbled sand-stone figure of a sea-goddess. Looking back through shrubs and flowers, I saw the Roman tower of the castle soaring far above me into the deep blue of the sky. The place was inexpressibly solitary, not a ship, not a sail to be seen. The wind had died away; the sea was a vast blue mirror; time was lost. I understood why Rainer had often been here. He had described the spot to me and told me that it was here he had made the first draft of the elegies. The elegies—which now he said he would never finish! I knew that he was walking up and down the terrace with Princess Marie, deep in talk. They had not met for a long time and had much to say to each other, so I left them alone.

But after lunch we spent an hour together, sitting in the open air, and the princess invited me to her room for a "little chat to get to know each other," as she said. We spent an interesting afternoon in the red room, of which she seemed very fond, for it was there that she assembled her guests for reading aloud, unless there was music. It had a handsome Venetian stucco ceiling with a painted centre-piece representing the apotheosis of Kaiser Leopold I. The colours were magnificent, and round the painting were cherubs, garlands of fruit and wreaths of flowers. The walls were covered with deep red velvet; a bluish-pink carpet, in which was repeated the pattern of flowers on the ceiling, covered the whole floor. There were a few comfortable chairs and low stools in front of a little cabinet containing valuable glass, old Viennese and Meissen porcelain, Sèvres vases and small objects of silver. Along the side wall was a big bookcase, inlaid with different-coloured woods. Heavy red silk cords looped back the curtains from the windows and on the walls were many pictures, chiefly by Venetian painters.

In this beautiful room the princess told me much of the history of the castle. I learned that in the Middle Ages Duino was called "Tybein". It was the property of a rich and powerful family, who held it as liegemen of the Patriarch of Aquileia. Later the Tybeins freed themselves from the supremacy of the patriarch and owed allegiance to the Babenberg Dukes of Austria. Aquileia espoused the cause of the Guelphs, the lords of Tybein that of the Ghibellines. Thus conflict broke out between them, and there were battles with Trieste, war with Venice.

In the thirteenth century the Tybein family died out; the

lordship of Duino fell to the Wallsees and, when in turn this family became extinguished, to the House of Austria. But the castle must have had its most brilliant period under Kaiser Friedrich III, for he held court at Duino, instituted great feasts, jousts and tournaments, and is said to have kept two poets laureate. Unfortunately the princess could not tell me the names of these chosen poets, but according to tradition Dante had stayed here when, as an exile and a fugitive, he had been entertained by the patriarch, Pagano della Torre. Count Thurn-Valsassina, an ancestor of the princess on her mother's side, bought Duino from Kaiser Leopold I, and it had thus been in the possession of her family for almost three hundred years.

I asked whether the name of Tybein had any definite meaning. There were ruins with a similar name—Theben on the River March, Devin on Lake Hammer in Bohemia. As a child I had often picnicked there. But the princess could tell me nothing of the origin of the name. I decided to ask Rilke whether the word came from the Indo-Germanic "devar", which means "prince". At home we once had a visit from an Indian of the kingly caste, whose lovely wife had been named "Devi", meaning princess. Was it possible that Devin-Tybein signified "house of princes"?

In the next few days I was promised a tour of the castle, in which there were innumerable halls, rooms, concealed nooks, dungeons, chambers and passages. But we were to wait until Pater Serafico, as the princess called Rilke, had recovered his strength. I took the risk of asking whether she found him changed, but she showed no anxiety, simply answering that the journey had tired him.

I do not think that anyone noticed at that time, except myself, that Rilke was showing the first symptoms of his illness, which later became so grave. They passed unnoticed, probably because no one observed his condition with enough attention. And he was so considerate of others that he concealed it with heroic self-control.

That evening we had guests—Tomaso della Torre, a near relative of the family, one or two ladies, a philosopher and an elderly American. Conversation turned to snake-charmers in Calcutta and ice-festivals in Finland. The talk was quick and vivacious, a ball-game in which witty, ironic remarks were tossed to and fro. Rilke took no part in it. He did not care for talk of that kind and I fully shared his dislike of it. He was sitting next to me, and I noticed that he ate little and hardly spoke at all. When we left the table to go up to the white room, he asked in a low voice whether I would play. I said that perhaps the mood of the party was not quite attuned to music, but the princess, who had joined us, cried vivaciously, "Yes, Serafico, she must play. Get her to play. I have heard enough about conjurers and ice palaces and I am longing for music!"

The white room was immediately above the dining-room. It was of the same size and had the same three huge windows, which afforded a lovely view of Trieste and the gulf. It differed from the dining-room, however, in having white and gilt furniture and light-coloured walls. There were no carpets, but under chairs and table were fine white skins on the beautifully inlaid parquet. The only dark object was a great Bösendorfer grand piano, on which Liszt had once played. His hands had raised the lid; his fingers had touched the keys! I hardly dared to begin. Then one of the men said half-jokingly to his neighbour, "Women cannot really play the piano, can they?"

As soon as I heard it I forgot the room and was conscious only of Rainer's face. I was back in the Andersen room, playing for him alone, as on that evening when I played the Beethoven Sonata opus 109.

When I had finished, I sat for a moment with closed eyes as was my habit. Then I felt two hands take hold of my shoulders from behind. Princess Marie had come up behind me and laid her face against my hair.

"Child, child," she said, almost inaudibly, but in a tone of deep emotion. I looked up to her, happy and grateful. Tears were shining in her grave, kindly eyes. I rose and kissed her hand, and my eyes sought Rilke, but I could not find him. The guest who had made the remark about women-pianists broke the silence by saying gravely, "Rilke has gone and why should we stay—we have heard the voice of God." I thanked him with a glance, but how perfect would my happiness have been if Rilke had only given me a look or a hand-clasp!

The company that had been so cheerful and high-spirited at dinner broke up almost with solemnity. I took my candle and went up the stairs alone. But before I reached my door, a dark

figure detached itself from a window recess. I made a startled
movement, the candle fell from my hand and went out. And so
we stood facing each other, Rainer and I. Only a faint shimmer
of the waning moon lay in the window-niche where he had stood
waiting for me. I could scarcely see him, but how deeply I was
aware of Fra Angelico's whole being, as he said, "O, my love,
how you played! One has not yet learned how to survive so much
splendour. Dear heart, how God must love you!"
Then he slipped away into the darkness.

(From the Diary.)

The beauty and peace of the landscape constantly transport
me into the dream atmosphere of long-past days. I often feel I
am living in some earlier century. I should hardly be surprised if,
on one of the many concealed paths among the laurels and holm-
oaks, I were suddenly to come upon a figure from the *rinascimento*.

Most days at Duino follow the same pattern. At eight o'clock a
girl brings my breakfast to my room; the morning is mine for
work, writing, reading or taking walks. At noon a bell rings in the
courtyard for the servants' lunch and they gather in their own
pleasant dining-room next to the kitchen. At one o'clock a gong
sounds for the family and guests. After lunch black coffee is
served on the terrace, then we take a siesta. At four o'clock we
generally go out for a car-ride in the vicinity, to Trieste, Gorizia
or Sistiana, or gather on the terrace again for tea. But the best
part of the day is the evening, when we have music or readings
in the white room or the red room.

Here the princess read to us Dante's *Vita nuova* in Italian.
Here I first heard Rilke read Hölderlin, one of his favourite poets.
He chose "Bread and Wine" and afterwards a very beautiful
poem to Morning. He rates Hölderlin first of lyric poets and
when I hear pieces like the "Rhine" or "Song of Fate"[1] I can
understand his enthusiasm.

Of his own works Rilke read the Czar cycle[2] and—what a
contrast!—some passages from the *Life of Mary*. The latter
work brought him into an extraordinary artistic relationship with
the painter, Heinrich Vogeler. He is going to tell me about it
when we are alone. But other people take up a great deal of his
time. Sometimes we see each other only at meals and in the

[1] "Schicksalslied".   [2] "Dei Zaren".   [3] *Marienleben*.

evening in the drawing-room or the gallery, when the whole party is present.

But occasionally of a morning we take a short walk to the post-office to post our letters. Mornings I practise pieces on the piano for my new programme, while Rilke works in the library. He is reading a great deal about Carlo Zeno, the Venetian sea hero, in whom he is greatly interested. There are contemporary pictures and documents about him here and also an old Life. The princess hopes—and I heartily agree with her—that Rilke will begin his long-planned work on Carlo Zeno before he leaves.

Yesterday the princess and her son, Prince Pascha, went to Grado with the American. The old man's Christian name is Horatio—"instead of William or John, which would suit him much better," says Rilke, who regards him as an eccentric. I can make nothing of Horatio; he is generally silent, sucking at the strongly-scented honey-dew in his English pipe. The princess says he has a great respect for Rilke "though he does not show it," but Prince Pascha is of the opinion that he knows nothing of poetry. Sometimes mother and son have amusing little discussions on the subject, in which Prince Pascha generally comes off best, producing unanswerable arguments that reduce his mother to silence.

Yesterday they went off with Horatio and were not expected back before evening. Rilke and I spent the whole afternoon by the stone goddess at the edge of the water. I had brought with me one of those little pieces of needlework of which Rilke is very fond—a white cambric handkerchief with a fine open-work hem. I was going to embroider the edges with tiny flowers in bright pink silk. He finds it agreeable and soothing to look on at this delicate work, so I do it sometimes, not only to provide birthday presents for Maria, but also to please Rainer. The other evening I was touched to find this passage on re-reading one of his letters: ". . . you do not know what it means to me to think I shall watch you embroidering bright silk flowers on white cambric—and if I take a book and read aloud to you and can therefore watch you no longer, there will be no place in my whole being that does not *know* you are embroidering silk flowers on white cambric, and that does not therefore retreat into its own sacred refuge, where it is almost impossible to remain mortal. Many years ago I spent a winter far away in the south in a villa

whence we could watch the sea across an evergreen garden.
There were only four of us, three women of diverse age and
myself—an old lady (the hostess), a widow (no longer young) and
a charming girl. . . . There were evenings (we had few visitors)
when we sat together in the big studio, close to the fire, the ladies
with their needlework, I with a book—and it always ended with
the girl peeling me an apple. . . .

"Will you believe me, Benvenuta, when I say that I lived for
years and years on that apple, which I had not had to provide
for myself, on those evening hours, on something that the nearness and gentle activity of those three women seemed to have
originated and collected within me? Yes, and much later, long
after my return to Paris, there was still a store of—(what?)—of
poise, of solace, of cooling assuagement inside me, and I knew by
the feel of it that it came from thence. And it was so real, so
tangibly stored up in me, that I could almost see it melt and
diminish under my daily, ever more niggardly expenditure. *And
then it was no more than a gesture,* and yet I was maintained by
it—think!—for years . . ."

"Even little things can delight us"[1]—so says one of Hugo
Wolf's loveliest songs from the Italian Songbook (I must show it
Rainer one day). Yes, Rilke knows "the soul of little things", as
he calls it—and loves it too.

And so we wandered down to our favourite spot, he with a
book, and I with a basket full of bright skeins of silk. Rilke
wanted to read me the final chapter of Knoop's book, which we
had not been able to finish in Paris. So we sat on the bench
looking over the sea, working and reading.

When we had finished, we spoke of forces of which men are
sometimes unconscious, forces that govern the soul and occasionally burst forth from it, as in that phantasmal work of
Knoop's, "The A and the O."

"Do you think," I asked, "that elements that are often completely unconscious can express themselves in the poet's mode of
creation?"

He gave me a long, thoughtful look. "You know, that is hard to
fathom. It is so, but it may also be quite different. Once in Paris
I read my very youthful poem, the 'Song of Cornet Christopher

---

[1] *Auch kleine Dinge können uns entzücken.*

Rilke', in an Italian translation (not that of our good Cecilia Bracchi)," he said with a little smile. "And in that rich, foreign, chivalrous language it drove right through my heart. I read it twice aloud in the deep silence of the room. The foreign language, for which I have such a liking, gave the poem back to me as though it rose surging anew in another blood. I thought of that windy, moonlit night when I wrote it, and I felt that then I had known the shortest way through my own heart. The early portrait of my father—you remember it?—may have suggested to me that those few lines on the *Cornet*, as they lay there before me, taken from my father's papers, could be used as a rocket, and it soared up at a spark from my heart's fire and described its bold, irresistible parabola in the spacious night of my presentience of life—in a dreamy, creative night, for literary production was not then a thing of such immeasurable responsibility. I did not then foresee how I should later admire those who die young, and the mild aspect of their deadness that is turned toward us. But later on in Rome, when, quite mysteriously, the imaginary figure of *Malte* first confronted me, I was shocked by the sudden realisation that he must die young."

"Did you also think of little Erik?"

Rilke went on as though he had expected my question: "Yes, when I invented little Erik and related him to Malte, it was this again that peculiarly concerned me: the durations and vacancies and fullnesses of childhood, which are accomplished without curtailment, even in a life *qui n'aura qu'un tout petit lendemain transparent.*"

He stopped and looked into the shining distance ahead of us. The sea was calm and opalescent in the evening sunshine; above us in the holm-oaks the birds were singing in the late, warm sunshine.

It was wonderful to hear Rilke speak; his best, most personal world was revealed again, homely, clear and tranquil.

"And then——?" I asked.

He turned his quiet face towards me. "I will tell you an odd story of unconscious creation: Heinrich Vogeler and I once decided to do a book together. It was to be my poems on the life of Mary; Vogeler was to make the drawings for it and I sent him the manuscript. It is a long time ago, and, thoughtless as young people are, I had made no copy of them. Months later Vogeler wrote me that he could not find the poems and I was to send him a copy. That was impossible. I had forgotten them and, after reflection it seemed to me that any attempt to write them down from memory was hopeless. I gave them up for lost and they remained so.

"Years later I spent months in Duino in complete solitude, splendidly alone, reading much, working little. One day, walking through the gardens—I was on my way to the 'sacred grove'—verses began to form in my mind. I took my note-book and wrote, read what I had written, and went on writing. Suddenly it all came back; how, I could hardly understand, but the songs of Mary became clear and vivid, happy, familiar, as though I had always known them."

We both fell silent, lost in the magic of that May day and of the strange incident Rilke had narrated. At last I asked, "Do you think they had, so to speak, been sleeping in your mind and been awakened?"

Rilke looked into the distance, and his eyes seemed to gaze far across the sea to some strange, undiscovered land. "No," he said softly, "for now comes the mystery: shortly afterwards Vogeler sent me the original manuscript, which by an odd chance had come to light. But the poems were quite different from those I thought I had remembered in the garden at Duino. When I read the originals again, they seemed colourless, almost insignificant—even the meaning was different. The authentic songs of Mary are therefore the ones I wrote down here, looking over the sea, without guessing that they were a quite new work."

I feel now that as a result of this wonderful story I have been able to gain fresh insight into the operation of Rilke's genius. And I cannot help thinking of one of his earlier poems which foreshadows not only this particular happening, transcending space and time, but perhaps his whole life:

> "This is my test,
> sworn to the quest
> each fleeting hour to know—
> then firm of breast
> a thousand rootstrings throw
> deep in life's clay—and so

through pain to climb
far out of life, and grow
far out of time"[1]

This year May is very lovely. The days are full of sunshine;
one longs to spend the warm nights out of doors watching the
nomad army of stars that pass across the sky, great, shining and
innumerable. In the evening, the first lights of Trieste gleam
across the bay, the dusk puts out all colours, melts the contours
into a soft grey and brings the first star twinkling in a dying, pale-
green sky. Then I often think of Rilke's poem "The Reader"[2].
Can there be anything more vivid than its opening lines:

"Long time I read while the declining day
with beating rain outside the windows lay,
I heard not how the wind the branches shook,
heavy my book . . ."[3]

And then the conclusion, in which the world becomes harmony
and fulfilment:

". . . The earth grows out beyond itself: afar
it seems to comprehend the whole of heaven,
till the last house is like the nearest star."[4]

The poem might well have been written here, but Rilke says
he had never been to Duino when he wrote it. It was the evenings
at Worpswede that found expression in that dream-picture.

[1] *"Das ist mein Streit*
sehnsuchtsgeweiht
durch alle Tage schweifen—
dann stark und breit
mit tausend Wurzelstreifen
tief in das Leben greifen—
und durch das Leid
weit aus dem Leben reifen,
weit aus der Zeit."
[2] *Der Lesende.*
[3] *"Ich las schon lang, seit dieser Nachmittag*
mit Regen rauschend vor den Fenstern lag,
vom Winde draussen hörte ich nichts mehr,
mein Buch war schwer. . . ."
[4] *". . . da wächst die Erde über sich hinaus.*
Den ganzen Himmel scheint sie zu umfassen:
der erste Stern ist wie das letzte Haus."

Not long ago, after a long talk about music and our musical evenings, I told the princess how nice it would be if the piano were on the terrace, so that one could play without going indoors.

She looked at Rilke with a peculiar smile, but neither answered. In the evening she remarked that a string quartette had often played at the castle for d'Annunzio, who was a passionate lover of music. I sighed and said longingly, "Heavens, how marvellous the Dvořák quintette would sound here!" At that the princess and Rilke again exchanged a significant glance. A little later Princess Marie said suddenly, "Yes. Five."

During our evening walk, when I was alone for a moment with Rilke, I asked him what that strange exclamation had meant, but again he only smiled. I was almost offended, for it seemed that he and the princess were discussing behind my back something they would not share with me, but two days later the carefully guarded secret was out.

Yesterday morning two motor-cars drove into the court-yard. A double-bass and a cello were unloaded from the first, and from the second alighted *five* men with violin cases—the Trieste string quartette and the double-bass player "for the Dvořák quintette", as the princess, noticing my surprise and delight, smilingly remarked.

We had a wonderful day of music. The leading violin, Herr Jankovitch, is a distinguished musician, and has trained his quartette magnificently. In the morning we played in the drawing-room, at first alone, to settle matters of tempo and ensemble, but in the afternoon Princess Marie had the grand piano wheeled out on to the terrace and the stands set up.

I believe that concert was the strangest and most unforgettable in my whole life.

The piano stood under a bower of roses and wisteria, with which the pergola is nearly smothered. A mass of purple, red and yellow buds, interlaced with full-blown flowers, hung along the whole length of the terrace. The air was full of the sweetest scents. And here we played Beethoven, Mozart, Schumann and Dvořák.

The surge of the sea came up to us; little birds among the flower-laden sprays sang their small, melodious solos in the midst of a scherzo or an adagio.

We could not stop playing, and our listeners did not tire. The sun went down, the sky turned golden, a light breeze shook the leaves of the pergola and tossed rose-petals on to the piano, and still we went on playing, till the first pale stars shone out in the sky and the rosy clouds paled over the sea.

It was a dream of flowers, music, scent and the songs of birds, set on a rock-based castle on the sea, against a background of enchanting country.

Finally the musicians played the *adagio* from a later string quartette of Beethoven: the last chords died out in the twilight with almost supernatural beauty.

When we gathered in the dining-room, that evening, there was much lively conversation. The princess was radiant, Rilke quite excited. He thought the Dvořák quintette unspeakably beautiful! "What invention! What spirit! What melancholy!" he cried, and was shocked when he heard that Dvořák had died insane. Someone observed that so many great men had been fated to die tragically, and I could not help thinking of what Rilke had once said about Beethoven: ". . . with his hearing even the last criterion was taken from him so that he could only surge like the primeval forest . . ."

About midnight the five musicians drove back to Trieste. As they were being shown out, I stayed behind in the hall for a moment with Rilke. He felt that the last movement of the quartette, with which the concert had ended, was more than "earthly language": it was a revelation of which we can only divine the meaning; it was the expression of a soul that has risen into other realms and tried to bring to the semi-darkness of our imperfect world a gleam of that unknown sphere of inner consecration and "uttermost bliss". I said it was an unparalleled cruelty of so-called fate that Beethoven had never been able to hear this music. "But he was *himself* this music," said Rilke, and his face had a solemn expression of peace and fulfilment, such as I had not seen on it for a long, long time.

He often anticipated unspoken questions, answering them almost unconsciously. So he said now, "There is so much to which we can never attain, so much that will never be granted to us. I often think of the monk in that Indian fable. Doesn't that help to make it all more comprehensible?"

Oh, dear, dear Rainer, if only everything were clearer and simpler in our own lives and our attitude to one another.

•   •   •   •   •   •   •

This morning we were in the castle gardens. Rilke showed me something of which Prince Pascha is very proud. That is the violet-*trees* that grow here, a unique horticultural achievement. The stems, nearly eighteen inches in height, bear thick green crowns of leaves with sweet-smelling flowers, light or dark in colour. How these little miracles are grown is the horticultural secret of Duino. They are planted in two rows in the sun outside the glass-house, like a miniature avenue, and the little tree-crowns actually throw shadows! These gardens are in a class by themselves. There are beds of early strawberries and seedlings under glass. Carrots, spinach and the famous Italian cauli-flowers are planted in neat rectangles. Peas and beans twine up tall sticks and in the glass-house orchids are cultivated, with carnations, cyclamen and every kind of beautiful palm and foliage plant. A delicious scent fills this warm moist world, and a little fountain plays in the middle of the floor, its spray falling into a stone basin where goldfish are swimming. The box-hedges out of doors are showing fresh shoots, and how simple and charmingly old-fashioned is the narrow, stone-paved path beyond, leading to the "sacred grove". It is shady there under the trees, but at the entrance, in the niche by the gate, little brown lizards sun themselves on a low wall.

Here something quite charming happened. Rilke is quite immersed in the life of nature; his love, his interest, go out to the tiniest things, which most people would pass unheeding.

We sat on the low wall and watched little red spiders, shimmer-ing green beetles and bright-winged, delicate, transparent insects threading their way between sun-warmed patches of moss and dry earth.

"Look," said Rilke, with quick attention, and pointed to a little black ant. It ran along the warm stone of the wall, scrambled bravely over his hand and hurried on as though absorbed in some quest. Now it had found a thin, dry, rolled-up petal. The ant seized it and tried unsuccessfully to push it along, for it was several times larger than the little insect. But the ant did not give up. With great exertion it dragged its prize a little farther and stopped as if to rest. But a light wind swept the petal away, leaving it far beyond the spot where it had first been discovered. Rilke had watched all this with great sympathy. "Should I help?"—"No," I said. "Think of your beetle that wanted to climb the grass-blade and fell down. Not even God could help, and we are only human. What would the ant think of us?"

Rainer was quite serious. "You are right," he said. "Perhaps it has an uncle or a sister-in-law that could help."

When we looked again the ant had vanished. Now I too was troubled. "It has given up," I said. But Rilke would not believe it. "No," he cried, "it has gone to fetch its uncle." We both laughed, and of a sudden the ant reappeared: it had brought both its uncle *and* its sister-in-law. The three seized the elusive booty with hasty resolve and in a few moments they had reached their goal—a crack in the wall. They carried the petal inside and disappeared, "like furniture-removers carrying a piano into a house," said Rilke, with a sigh of relief at the happy conclusion of the enterprise.

At midday he told the princess the story of the ant. She laughed. "You are a pair of fantastic children," she said, in the charming Austrian dialect she liked to assume in moments of gaiety, "but I understand. As a child I made friends with all sorts of creatures in the 'sacred grove', and I'm sure your ant's great-grandmother was one of them, Serafico."

The talk turned to popular books, which, as Prince Pascha remarked, suit the taste of Nietzsche's *Vielzuviele* and are bought, read, praised and recommended on all sides. Rilke thought it shocking, but the princess disagreed; the masses read only rubbish; great and important works had always had difficulty in establishing themselves. A small group of really high-minded, artistic people had always had to teach the rest of the world what is great and significant.

The American did not agree. He said that truly great art was understood by all.

The princess laughed. "But do you think that Goethe's fame was established by the approval of the multitude, or that my coachman in Lautschin can appreciate the quality of Beethoven's symphonies? The general public decides, does it? It has always been the enemy of our geniuses. It has to be educated by individuals, so far as it can be educated at all. If one person says to another, 'That is beautiful,' and can say it with enough force, many others come in time to believe it—and then perhaps they really like it. But the public has never thought of it for themselves. We should have to be very much on our guard if the masses had to decide whether a Schopenhauer is great or not. His works were used to wrap up cheese, yes, and sausage for servant-girls. And Bach was almost forgotten for a hundred years until one person, Felix Mendelssohn, re-discovered him and brought him back to light."

But the American was not to be converted. He thought it was not quite fair to attribute culture only to a certain class. I believe that at that moment Rilke must have been thinking of Marthe and of her fervent longing for what is great and beautiful. He looked sadly at the princess, but she shook her head and turned back to the American. "Dear Horatio, you don't understand what I mean. Humanity is not divided into watertight compartments. For talent or genius there is no such thing as class; everything depends on personality. Our great Beethoven, the friend of so many princes, was the son of a drunken scoundrel and a maidservant, or such-like. If the son of my housekeeper were a genius, I would certainly help him to make a career. And, by the way, the old Princess Reuss invites her former gardener's apprentice to play in a quartette in her house, for he has become an excellent violinist. But for the public, the masses—my stable boys and kitchen-maids and milkmaids—to have a voice in deciding whether our Pater Serafico is a great poet or not—you simply cannot get that into my old head."

Everyone laughed. Even the American had to smile; he accepted defeat and fell into his habitual silence. The princess went on, turning to the others: "Only one must be thoroughly consistent and, for instance, respect a cobbler as cobbler, so long as he is a good workman and a decent fellow. But you cannot expect him to read the *Divina Commedia*; it would only bore him to death. After all, there must be different classes in society; God arranged matters so, and we shall not be able to change it."

With that she rose from the table. Rilke, who had listened attentively to the princess's little speech, kissed her hand. He remarked that if the problem of international understanding could everywhere be solved in this way, there could be no question of universal decadence, which we were told would overtake us in the far future, but rather of an eternal progression.

The others went to their rooms, Rilke and I strolled down through the garden to our favourite spot by the sea. I expressed my admiration for the broad-minded, humane and far-sighted views of the princess, and Rilke said that the freedom of her mind was all the more surprising since she had been brought up in a rigid, feudal tradition by her mother, who was proud, aristocratic and a strict Catholic. But even when she was little Princess Hohenlohe, she had had an irresistible impulse toward freedom and an understanding of people and art far in advance of the conventions and traditions of her class. He had realised this when reading her early diaries, and he added that he owed much to her ripe judgment.

Then, for the first time after a long interval, he spoke again of the elegies, and said he would read them aloud to us. If I had not known in my inmost heart how deep and genuine, how pure and great, is his conception of his vocation as a poet, I could not have learned it better than from what he said now. Stimulated by the conversation at lunch, we talked of good and bad books, of poets and their duty to their work. Rilke mentioned a passage in Caroline von Schelling's letters, where she says that good fruits can never again be expected of those who have once borne bad. I asked if this judgment were not too severe, for many people had the good will to correct their mistakes.

"But, you see," he retorted, "I do not mean it like that. I mean the level of art one is capable of producing, for (I believe I have said this to you once before), if any artist is satisfied with something below his present best, he is lost for the greatest. If ever I thought of such a person, I was always full of horror at those who produce their minimum, with the left hand, so to speak, using some exhausted remnants of vitality, under the impression that later on, when they have a mind to it, they can again produce something good."

I once heard a writer of some reputation remark that he had sometimes to get himself into the mood before he could work. Rilke thought such an attitude a desperate one. He said that some writers thought they must write at all costs; they wanted to juggle, "like the Indian conjurers, who make a plant grow in a moment under an upturned pot . . . I never wanted to be a juggler," he said. "I never wanted a potion that could make my blood lustrous like a poison flower; I never wanted my heart to swell with the fermentation of liquors poured into it; when it surged upward, it was by the irresistible laws of the ocean tides, and when I was inspired, it was by the intangible and noble spirit that cannot be summoned or petitioned." He put his hand on my arm and, as he looked at me, his eyes seemed to shine with an inner light. "Benvenuta," he said, "I speak to God in you. To you I *can* say it. In a human sense my life is somehow forfeit. *I know it.* But my art is pure. In my house the golden columns stand like the boles of forest trees, and in the figures on the curtains there is not a thread that is not beautiful with the purest colours. How God must have stood by me, for me to be able to say that!"

He breathed deeply and leaned back as though to let the sea wind cool his face. "Thank you," I said. I could not hide from him the tears in my eyes. Silently we sat there in the blossoming splendour; silently we went back presently through the little paths to the castle, where reality was waiting for us.

Princess Marie was standing at the gateway in cloak and motoring cap. "I'm glad you have come," she called out to us. "They have been searching everywhere for you. Would you like to come to Aquileia? The car is waiting."

We had been by car to Gorizia and Sistiana, a delightful little bathing resort that belongs to Princess Marie. We had admired the new gardens and the lovely views. We had driven through Opčina to Trieste, where I had a very pleasant afternoon and played at the Hohenlohe's. But of all our excursions the one to Aquileia was the strangest, the saddest and the most sinister.

The drive across the Isonzo to Ronchi and Monfalcone was delightful. On our arrival Rilke and I had seen nothing but darkness and rain, but this time the landscape was bathed in bright sunshine. The Gulf of Trieste was as though embedded in light; the inlets and the far islands shone in the early afternoon sun. As we came to a little village, the princess showed us the beautiful park and villa of the former Empress Eugénie of France. Then we followed an apparently endless road, dead straight and with a very bad surface, through a stony region dotted with rubble and deserted houses, to Aquileia.

When you see the few, mostly gloomy and poverty-stricken dwellings, you can hardly believe that this is the site of one of the greatest cities of antiquity. We walked down a little lane, in which stood a few of the better houses, and reached the cathedral.

There the princess showed us the mosaic floor which had recently been discovered and laid bare beneath the more modern stone floor. We descended almost the depth of a room, through rubbish that had been only partially cleared away, to reach the ancient floor of the church. The mosaics, wonderfully preserved, are nearly seven hundred years old, Rainer says. They are in beautiful colours and show carpet-patterns, allegories, pictures of saints and certain figures that look very heathen—a warrior, a goddess of victory. The patriarchs della Torre, Princess Marie's ancestors, are buried in the cathedral chapel of St. Ambrosius. She told us that for hundreds of years the so-called *Cantus patriarchinus* has been sung at High Mass and that it is not allowed to be sung in any other church in the world. The cathedral was granted this privilege in early Christian times, probably by St. Ambrosius.

But who in these days hears this ancient, mystical hymn? A few poor women, the owner of the little shop at the street-corner, a few local children? The decline is depressing.

While the others were still in the cathedral, Rilke and I walked about among the old gravestones outside, among the remnants of columns and the ruins of palaces long since destroyed. Rilke has often been here. He is attached to this mysterious countryside and loves the graveyard, where grow the largest and finest cypresses I have ever seen. He says that on this spot once stood the palace of the Emperor Augustus, where he entertained King Herod of Judæa, who had dared the long and perilous journey across the sea—God knows why!—to visit him.

The history of this long dead and demolished town is a grisly one, full of blood, murder and conflict. But out of the ruins one can conjure up the happenings of thousands of years, as though, looking back in a waking dream, one had taken part in them.

Like a present symbol of eternal suffering, a young priest lives here who was present at the great earthquake of Messina and was driven insane by the experience. Rilke told me that sometimes of an evening heart-rending screams and wails can be heard far off on the country roads. The unhappy man is looked after by two nuns.

The rest of the party came out of the church. The princess decided to drive straight home and I was glad to be able to leave that depressing place. We got into the car and Aquileia had soon

disappeared like a grisly dream. A cold wind blew in from
the sea and it was growing dark. We were all glad and somehow
relieved when at last the lighted windows of Duino greeted us in
the distance.

The pleasant stay at Duino had strengthened Rilke so much
that the attacks of fever and headache had ceased, but he grew
more and more taciturn and slept very late in the morning,
rarely leaving his room before noon. It really seemed as though
he would do no more work. He had not been in the library for a
long time, and he had given up studying the papers relating to
Carlo Zeno. Sometimes he still read aloud to us in the evenings,
generally Hölderlin, but occasionally his own translations, André
Gide and the gloomy but glowing letters of Marianna Alcoforado.
He buried himself in books and ideas remote from the world and
inimical to life, and for the first time we became somewhat
estranged from each other. Outwardly there was little sign of
this, for its vibrations were hardly perceptible, but it had its
predestined source in the direction of our two lives. The
occasion was this: Rilke had received some coloured pictures of
dolls—I believe from the woman who had made them. They
looked as though they had been modelled on insane persons or
on those sick from taking opium. He showed them me and I
thought them frightful. I was shocked when Rilke said he found
them "moving and beautiful". I answered, "The test of a toy is
whether children like it. But any healthy and innocent little girl
would be scared by these horrors."

I can still see Rilke's eyes grow quite dark, as always when he
was convinced of something. He said, almost beseechingly,
"But look, in their lives there are, so to speak, no children. They
are adults grown up from their own doll-childhood. They have
outgrown children's comprehension and begun, as it were, their
own independent life." I said that this doll-childhood and its
relation to children must have something very odd about it, if
from the idea of a harmless plaything could arise the monstrous
idea of a non-plaything. But Rilke became almost vehement. "A
toy gets worn out and bad!" he cried. "Don't say that the
badness of a toy is innocent. It needs all the unbounded innocence of children to keep permanently harmless all that is
dirty and depraved in a toy. Just imagine that such an object had

become deformed and depraved in the hands of adults—it would fill you with unspeakable loathing."

He went on to maintain that the dolls one had played with in childhood were soulless, while these revolting "grown-up dolls" had souls. I disagreed with him completely. The first doll I remember was given me on my third birthday. Her little peasant dress had an odour of hemp and upturned soil; her apron was red as a clover-field and her hood had a border of daisies. She shared my childhood's secrets. I told her my joys and sorrows, of which the grown-ups knew nothing, and she always understood.

"But that was due to you," Rilke objected. "You imagined her soul, a doll's soul. In your creative zest you gave her your own soul and then it was inside her, but only through you."

"Rainer," I said, "I cannot follow these intricate ideas. But I believe that what you say is a distortion of good, simple, healthy reality." But Rainer was seized with a genuine passion to make me understand him. He fetched a pamplet down from his cupboard—it was a number of *Weisse Blätter*—and began to read:

". . . since they are fed on imaginary food like the 'ka', reality, when they have to be brought in contact with it, only clogs and spoils them; they are impenetrable, proof in the most extreme and obvious degree, unable to admit at any point a single drop of water; they are without individual judgment, submissive to any numskull, and yet, once he becomes their property, possessing him in a very special way; they are lazy, complacent, unclean— dragged through the changing emotions of the day, left prostrate in each, sharing confidences, innocent or guilty, like a dog, but not receptive and forgetful like a dog; always a burden; initiated into the first nameless experiences of their owners, lying about in their earliest eerie loneliness, as though in empty rooms, as though nothing mattered but rudely, with every limb, to exploit the new spaciousness; dragged into children's beds, mislaid in the deep folds of diseases, appearing in dreams, involved in the fatalities of fevered nights: such were those dolls. For whatever happened they never exerted themselves; they lay there on the verge of a child's slumber, filled at most with the rudimentary fear of tumbling, letting themselves *be* dreamed, just as by day they were tirelessly ready to let themselves be lived with another's energy."

Perhaps Rilke felt my strong resistance. He paused. "Shall I
go on reading?"

I nodded, for I wanted to hear and know whether he would
find a way out, a reassuring gleam. He went on:

". . . when one considers how grateful objects are for
tenderness, how it helps them to recover, yes, how even the
hardest usage, always provided one loves them, seems to them an
exhausting caress, beneath which they shrink but acquire, as it
were, a heart—when one considers this, and remembers what
sensitive beauty certain objects can assume when they have been
drawn deeply and warmly into human life—and I do not mean
even that one need walk through the halls of the 'Almeria' in
Madrid, wondering at the armour, helms, daggers and two-handed
swords, in which the pure, wise art of the armourer has been
infinitely surpassed by something which the proud and fiery use
of these weapons has superimposed on them—I will not speak of
the warmth, the pathos, the forsaken-contemplative quality of
many objects, whose beautiful habituation to human life has
moved me in passing. Let me quickly name quite simple things
—a distaff, a spinning-wheel, a domestic loom, a bride's glove, a
cup—not to speak of the great will of the hammer, the surrender
of a violin, the good-humoured zeal of horn-rimmed spectacles.
. . . If one called to mind all these objects and found at the same
time one of our dolls—extracting it from a heap of more co-
operative things—we should be almost enraged by its terrible,
sleek forgetfulness; the hatred, which, unconsciously, always
formed part of our attitude towards it, would burst forth, and the
thing would lie before us unmasked, a horrid alien object on
which we had wasted our purest affection; the dripping, super-
ficially bedizened corpse, which let itself be lifted and borne by
the floods of our tenderness, till we were dry again and left it
lying in some bush."

I had listened with a strange dual feeling of admiration and
regret. Again I was firmly held by his unmatched ability to
present and interpret things. And yet the shadow of a hostile
thought lay over all the beauty.

". . . I can only imagine that there were certain over-long
afternoons when we tired of our mutual conceits, and suddenly
found ourselves sitting opposite a doll, expecting something from
it. Perhaps there lay near-by one of those things that are ugly

and stinted by nature and therefore full of ideas of their own, the head of a Punch that refused to be smashed, a half-broken horse or something that made a noise and yet could not hope by any effort of its own to drown our noise and that of the whole room . . . but if there was nothing there to distract our thoughts, if that inactive creature went on sprawling, heavily, obtusely, like a rustic Danaë, knowing nought but the incessant golden rain of our invention—I wish I could remember whether we then rebelled, sprang up and told the monster that our patience was exhausted; whether we did not face it, trembling with rage, and ask what use it made of all our warmth . . . then it was silent, for that was its constant subterfuge, because it was made of worthless, utterly irresponsible stuff—silent, not even thinking of exploiting the situation, of procuring some benefit from it, in a world where fate, even God himself, have made a name largely by the silence they maintain towards us. . . . May it not be that a doll is still malevolently at work in this person or that, making him pursue vague satisfactions, simply as a result of the dissatisfaction with which it has ruined his disposition? I remember seeing an old hereditary doll in the hands of the children at the manor-house of a remote Russian estate. It bore a resemblance to the whole family . . . but I will tell you why we did not make an idol of you, you stuffed rag, and did not go down in fear of you—it was, I tell you, because we had in mind something quite different, something invisible; we had in mind a soul: the doll-soul.

". . . Great, brave soul of the rocking-horse, that agitated the nursery air as if it were rocking over the famous battlefields of the world, proud, trustworthy, almost visible soul. You shook the walls, the window-frames, the daily horizons, you made them totter, as though the storms of the future were shaking those most temporary surroundings, that yet could take on such an invincible air in the dead slowness of afternoons. Oh, how you carried one out and away, rocking-horse soul, into the irrestibly heroic, where one went down hotly and gloriously, with shockingly dishevelled hair. Then you lay there, doll, and had not enough innocence to comprehend that your St. George was rocking beneath him the beast of your obtusity, the dragon that congealed inside you, our most fluid feelings producing a perfidious, indifferent infrangibility . . . at last no one held you and you were trodden underfoot . . ."

Suddenly I had an irrepressible desire to cry. "Rainer," I said, "I cannot listen any more. Forgive me, but it hurts me. It is very silly and childish of me, and I don't even know why your hatred of dolls affects me so much, for after all it is your hatred, not mine—but I cannot go on. I find it horrifying. It is not a matter of the literary quality of this essay, for it is exceptionally fine, it is probably because I cannot bear to hear the simplest, most innocent feelings and pleasures destroyed and picked to pieces. Do you understand me?"

He looked at me with a sad, almost helpless smile that went to my heart. Then I got up and crossed to the piano. I had to liberate myself. I was glad to sink into the pure tones of a Bach fugue, as though into the sacred stream of life.

When I had finished, I looked round: Rilke's chair was empty.

In Duino life went on as usual. My diary at this time consists merely of brief entries, such as: With the princess and Rilke on the terrace this morning, then played. Rilke feels strongly the value of silence after listening—no one knows so well as he how to listen. He is so fond of Chopin's Funeral March that he says he thinks it one of the most perfect works of art. Chopin, he says, put the whole tragedy of his life into this truly immortal melody; it is like his destiny, dark and sublime.

"Tragedy". This word recurred again and again. It made me desperate. I fought against it. It confronted me everywhere. And then came a fateful evening. It is thus recorded in my diary:

Today Rilke read aloud some fragments of the elegies. They are an image of himself as he now is—or always was? Who knows?

I cannot possibly think that he will not complete them. I can understand that this work, born of suffering, probably demands the final renunciation of all safe, warm, human life. I understand now what he means when he makes the sailor's bride bid him go because it is his fate to live in danger in strange and alien lands.

The poem made a deep impression on me, but I also felt its complete hostility to life, and my whole mind resisted it. I lay awake and asked myself desperately in the darkness why a poet who can understand humanity so profoundly should glorify doubt, fear, renunciation, resignation. Where is life's Yes, the courage to fight one's way to the light, the shining hope of victory? Do I betray Rainer by such thoughts, him, Fra Angelico, once my beloved voice of solace? . . . That is it—"once". For now I cannot help realising that he constantly expresses himself in terms of sadness and tragedy because he can do no other. What has become of his flaming enthusiasm, his rich humour, his joy?

Yes, everything has changed. When we are together I still feel his presence as something great and infinitely beautiful, but it seems to me that a spirit is gaining ground in him that drives him more and more towards negation. I feel it in everything we say to each other. There used to be, side by side with the gloom, so much that was gay and bright. Now the gloom has become a threat. Am I myself to blame that so much is unclear? Should I have the courage to speak openly about ourselves and the future? But am I so sure of being able to say something final?

The princess knows—dear, motherly woman that she is—that there is a shadow between Rainer and me which cannot be dispelled. If attacked, it would melt only to reform as a still denser fog.

Our stay at Duino was approaching its end. Princess Marie wished to visit her friends in Venice, in whose old palace on the Canal San Vio she had a little pied-à-terre, consisting of a few rooms. She had planned that we were to spend a week together in Venice. And now a series of distressing vacillations began. In the morning Rilke decided to go; in the evening he decided to stay; then he said he would follow, then asked whether we would postpone our departure and go with him later. Not an hour passed but something was decided and cancelled again. At last the princess resolved to go on ahead with me and leave Rilke to follow as and when he chose.

Departure from Duino! No, life had not grown brighter there, as I had so fervently wished and hoped when we left Paris. The anxious future had only hidden itself for a few hours in those radiant days of sunshine; the light had concealed and denied it. The day had swept away uneasy thoughts, but now that I was about to take leave of the place they returned to oppress my heart.

The day before our departure it rained, the garden was swept by a storm and we could not go out. Our trunks were brought down, Annina packed my things and the princess gave the servants instructions as to what they should do during her absence. Rilke, the princess and I spent the whole morning in the white room. I played for about an hour, but Rilke was silent and depressed. The reason for this I discovered later, for when we were alone he showed me a letter from his mother which had come by the early post. She addressed him as *"Du Prachtmensch"*[1], told him of some devotional exercises in which she had taken part at the nunnery, and wrote of the saint to whom she particularly entrusted his spiritual welfare; she begged him "not to be lukewarm in the true piety of a zealous Catholic", and reminded him to send her a parcel of gloves to clean, which he had evidently forgotten. He was to remember that it was her exclusive privilege to wash his gloves!

I gave him back the letter without a word. What could I say? As he folded it up and put it in his note-case, he said, scarcely audibly and as though asking a question, ". . . Mother?"

It hurt me unspeakably to see him pass his hand, almost as in forgiveness, across the pages written to him by this woman, this stranger, who "happened to bring me, of all people, into the world," he said.

Then he spoke of his father, to whom he still clung with what remained of a half-yearning, half-disillusioned gratitude. When Rainer was a child, his father always brought back a toy from his journeys, but Rainer was not allowed to see it. It disappeared at once into a mysterious cupboard that was always kept locked. When Christmas came his father also disappeared into the mysterious room that held the cupboard, and afterwards built a fabulous pile of presents in the drawing-room of their house in Prague. In the evening, when the tree was lit up, the most wonderful toys—rocking-horses and books, games and boxes of bricks—were heaped on the white-spread table reserved for presents.

"At that time he had no deep anxiety about you?"

Rilke had to smile. "No, we often went for walks together, my father and I, when I was very small. First I saw the silver crook of his stick from beneath, then, as I grew bigger, I could look down on it from above. But then our walks ceased altogether

---

[1] "You grand fellow".

and the endless years at the military academy of St. Pölten began. I thought at first that the saint who hid behind the unusual name of 'Pölten' must be a mysterious and cruel man, for 'Pölten' was not to be found in any legend, however much one searched the histories of saints and martyrs.''

Those desolate years came back to his mind. "Everything had to be shared, every game, every opinion, every thought, every aim, every obedience. We were not allowed to have a life of our own, a life that made demands on us, that called and ripened inside us. So every day I rose secretly at the first grey of dawn and sat—how often and bitterly I froze on cold winter mornings—at a window in the long corridors—just to be *alone* for a few stolen, precious moments, to think alone, to escape from that terrible, annihilating, inane community, in which one was utterly lonely and excluded.''

After five years came liberation and with it his first attempts to write. On one occasion, when he was seventeen, Rilke had to give up a piece of homework at his school.[1] He brought it printed in the *Prager Abendblatt*. The teacher was furious. "What is the meaning of this?'' he cried. "Are you trying to play a stupid joke on me?'' But Rilke bowed modestly and answered that his essay on the set subject, "Pen and Sword'', had really been printed in the evening paper.

The gloomy mood of departure had now brightened a little. Rilke even wished to make up for lost time by conducting me on the oft-postponed tour of the castle. So after lunch we set out. Many of the rooms I had never entered, and I could not understand the ease with which he found his way through all those passages, corridors, alcoves, communicating rooms, halls and galleries. But he told me that when the princess was away and he was living here alone, he had often wandered about the castle and had made some interesting discoveries. These had spurred him on to further search. He knew every picture; he knew the legend of the White Lady of Duino and the unhappy accursed priest who had to read mass at midnight once a year, wearing his blood-stained canonicals, in an underground chapel. And really there were so many secret doors, buried passages, nooks and crannies that it was not surprising if superstitious minds invented such grisly stories.

[1] *Gymnasium.*

In a large room in the unoccupied wing, where the curtains were generally drawn, many over-life-size portraits of the family of the Lords of Milan were hanging in half-darkness—Gerido, Pagano and Ludovici, who had gone on fighting the Viscontis in the thirteenth century until they were defeated and lost Milan and the iron crown. I did not know what the iron crown was, but Rilke told me it was the so-called "Lombard crown", a gold circlet, set with diamonds and precious stones, with thin iron bands inside it. According to tradition, the Kaiserin Helena had brought it back from Palestine and the iron bands were from a nail of the cross of Christ. The Lords of Milan had been crowned with this "*corona ferrea*". Now it was preserved in the cathedral at Monza.

Among these huge pictures, mostly quite badly painted, I was struck by one portrait. It represents a man with bold eyes, clothed in a scarlet cloak that enhances his black hair and wild features, and mounted on a horse that seems to leap out of the canvas. In the Taxis family he is called "*conte diavolo*" and many tales of adventure and mad escapade have been woven around him. Rilke told me one of the maddest. It was said to have happened in the rooms and the passage we had just left.

The "devil's count" had been condemned to death for some crime and was held in Duino awaiting execution. On the evening before he was to die, he invited the officers and soldiers of the guard to a farewell feast, which developed into a wild carouse. The count retired to his suite in repentant mood to prepare himself for the morrow, leaving his drunken guests asleep on and under the tables and chairs and about the floor. They were awakened at dawn by the loud report of a shot, rushed to the window and saw the count sailing out in a boat before the morning breeze. He vanished before their horrified eyes like a phantom of air.

Others claimed that they had seen the count's charger awaiting its master at the foot of the cliff and afterwards galloping with him across the wild, stormy sea to Aquileia, where horse and rider disappeared for ever.

Rilke showed me the door to a secret passage, which has now collapsed, and the trap-door through which the *conte diavolo* is said to have escaped.

We also inspected the little, airy chapel, a wonderful winding stairway designed and built by Palladio, early Venetian stucco ceilings, and a gallery wherein were painted the coats-of-arms of all the owners of Duino. Finally we walked back across the beautiful baroque terrace at the foot of the tower to the inner courtyard, whence we had set out. The statues and balustrades were streaming with rain. The little stone dolphin threw its thin jet feebly into the air, where it was seized and disintegrated by the falling veils of rain. Despite the many wonderful things we had seen, the day was dreary and sad.

In the evening, Rilke read aloud a few poems by Stefan George. The princess did not ask me to play and I had no desire to do so. She looked grave and thoughtful and kissed me with unusual warmth as she bade me good-night. Soon all the castle was still, but for some time my thoughts remained awake.

Venice

WE left early next morning. The rain had stopped but the air was cold. Milk-white mist covered sea and land. We wrapped ourselves in warm rugs and I gratefully accepted the loan of a fur coat from the princess. We led the way in an open car, while the maid followed in a second car with the luggage. The bright green tips of the trees rose spectrally out of the mist, dropped behind as we passed the spinney of beeches that lined the road. The castle itself, the battlements, Dante's rock, all the dear, familiar spots were lost to sight. The air had a tang of salt water and fresh foliage. It was as though Duino had ceased to be, extinguished like a dream.

We drove on in silence. Once the princess remarked: "It is a good thing Serafico overslept. If he had seen us go, he would have been sorry not to be with us."

I made no answer. I saw it all before me with too painful a clarity. Shortly before we left, as I was about to put the last little things into my bag, there was a knock at the door and Rainer asked if he could come in for a moment. He too must have slept badly, for his eyes were bright and feverish. He brought a gift that moved me to the heart. It was the ink-pot he had used when writing *Malte* and the little mat of brown, gold-blocked leather on which it had stood. I had often seen them on his writing-desk in Paris and he knew I had a special liking for them.

He said they would be better looked after with me than with him. But he had something else to say. He stood at the window, looking out at the veiled landscape, and began to speak. "I told you once I should pass out of your kindness into your patience, as from one room to another, as though I could go where I liked and lay my face in the flowers you have left and pass my hand over the silk of your dear feelings. But I shall never be able to tell you what you have done for me. God alone should give word to all gardens to tell you of it in their own blessed way; the stars, when you look up to them, should lay it, all heavenly and pure, in your heart. Do you know that? But what have I done? I have piled the heavy stones of my grief upon your joy, I have set my failing, withering life beside your confident hope and disappointed it, I have taken your flowers in my hand and they are faded. I thought I could give you my life, but my life is forfeit and has turned to your hurt. Can you forgive it all?"

I saw him turn, saw his beloved face in front of me and laid my head on his shoulder.

"Rainer," I said, shaken with sobs, "you must know how deeply and endlessly I thank you for everything, even the bitterest, because you let me have a share in all that moved your heart, in all the brightness and the blackness. Don't you feel that? Have I been unable to show it, that you can doubt it?"

And he said, overflowing, "Dear heart, O heart, even now you can still give, you dear beloved heart!" Then he was gone. The thought of this farewell filled me completely. I saw in a dream that the mist had gone, and we were driving at last through sunny country, across a little, dark-green river, through a small town with arboured walks, past an old city-wall by a moat, where great white callas were growing. Then we were back on a long straight road—the road to Mestre.

We reached Venice at midday. The princess's gondola was waiting outside the station. She alighted at the Campo San Vio, ordering the gondolier to take me to the Hotel Bristol, where she had reserved a room for me. "Till noon tomorrow at my place," she said. Then I was alone, alone for the first time for months, with my heavy, tormenting thoughts.

I found my mail awaiting me—a dear, though rather anxious letter from my old father, and one from Maria, asking me to come and stay with her. So the afternoon passed with writing. I wrote my sister that probably I should soon be with her. Then I went out to post, and the letter was almost a resolve and a decision.

Venice was full of life and gaiety. It was Saturday and many people had come in from the surrounding islands. Olive-brown children were sitting on the little marble lions, the *leoncini* of the Piazzetta, stroking the stone beasts and fighting for the privilege of riding them. Girls in their best clothes with fringed silk shawls walked arm-in-arm, singing softly and enjoying the mild evening, along the *riva*. Outside the cafés on the Piazza San Marco happy people were sitting over ices and lemonade. *Sabaione* was served in silver cups, and beggars and vendors of picture postcards moved through the dense crowd, crying their wares in sing-song voices. When quite a young girl I had paid a visit to Venice with my parents and had been enraptured by the life there. Now it hurt me—I could not help thinking of Duino left behind. Where was Rainer? Was he at our seat by the sea? Was he in his room, alone and thoughtful, as I was here? Or was the silent old butler serving his dinner at the long, empty table in the dining-room?

That night a storm blew across the lagoons. The windows shook, the waves slapped noisily on the stone steps of the old palaces, flag-staffs creaked and the chains of the moored gondolas groaned outside the house-doors. What a storm must have been raging at Duino! "Rainer, God preserve you!" I cried into the darkness. Then sleep came and took all care into its keeping and sank me into oblivion.

Next morning I went to hear the music at the Sunday service in San Marco. Priests in red, gold-embroidered robes, choir-boys in their white lace surplices, incense, altar-vessels gleaming in the light of hundreds of candles, provided a wonderful picture, and, with the glittering and diverse colours of the mosaic, the mighty arches wedding the pillars of the vast church to the domes soaring above them, made a strange and indescribable impression on me.

They sang the Marcellus mass of Palestrina, that A cappella mass without organ or instruments, written in the strict style of the old masters. Set against the shining splendour of gold and colour in this Byzantine church, it was like a severe sermon by Savonarola. I tried to follow the music, but my thoughts wandered repeatedly to Duino. Was Rilke sick? Would he follow us? What was going to happen?

Back in my hotel, I found a very sad letter from home. I read it over and over again, sitting on the quiet terrace by the canal, wondering wretchedly what answer, what comfort, I could send. Suddenly from the water the soft call of a gondolier caught my ear, coming from the happy crowds in the *vaporetti*. "*Sia di lungo*—keep straight on," he cried to an approaching gondola. I looked up: Rilke was there in the gondola, waving to me. Then it

K

had turned the corner, making for the hotel entrance. He was here! Happy and excited, I thought for a moment, while my heart beat fast, "Now everything is all right again." Then he appeared on the terrace, tired and feverish, and my pleasure changed abruptly to anxiety.

He did not wish to come to the princess's for lunch. He wanted only a cup of broth and two hours' rest. Yes, the storm had been quite terrible last night—not a moment's sleep—and then the journey in the crowded Sunday train. "But this afternoon I will show you Venice—my Venice, you know, the quieter one, of which strangers know so little. Yes, I shall be all right. I have been looking forward to it, all yesterday and all through my sleepless night. Do not be anxious, dear. Only a little rest, then call for me, please, at four o'clock or a little earlier."

We looked at each other and smiled. The birthdays of Rainer's childhood, of which he had told me so often, came back to our minds again. "Come at four o'clock or rather a little earlier."

At lunch I told the Taxis that Rainer had arrived. The princess was pleased and surprised. "I should not have been astonished if a telegram had suddenly come from him in Siena or Perugia. Sometimes he disappears all of a sudden and reappears where you least expect him, does he not, Titi?"

The princess's young cousin and a Baron Franchetti lunched with us, two amiable and interesting people. A sincere friendship grew up later between Titi Taxis-Metternich and myself, and survived through good and evil times. Rilke had told me in Duino about Franchetti, the owner of the famous *Ca' d'oro*. The princess was very fond of him and called him the last aristocrat of Venice. He was known as a great connoisseur of the arts, a most cultured, charming man and an excellent pianist, who had toured as a concert-artist. He had a very fine private collection of pictures, but it was scattered among the different rooms of the *palazzo* and so was not available to the public. He himself occupied—according to Rilke—two small rooms on the top floor; they were simply furnished, but contained several very beautiful pictures. This unusual man, half eccentric, half cavalier of the great world of yesterday, made an extraordinarily favourable impression. He was of middle height and had a calm, intelligent face, framed in a short beard. The thin, sinewy fingers of his very well-kept hands betrayed the pianist. His bearing and way of speaking proved him to be a descendent of distinguished Venetian families, and he upheld the tradition of his forefathers by his great love for his native city. He very rarely left Venice, and then only when urgent business required it.

We spoke of his collections. Most of his treasures he had inherited, but some he had acquired. He said in his low, courteous voice, bowing slightly, that he would be honoured if the princess and her guests would come to tea with him very soon in his simple apartment; he could then show us over the whole palace and we should see "a few interesting things", as he modestly put it. He had recently acquired two valuable Renaissance medallions—I think by Matteo de' Pasti—which would interest Rilke, if he would care to come along.

A little later I talked with Titi Taxis about music. She had been a pupil of Sarasate. Unfortunately she had left her violin in Berlin, but she warmly invited me to come in the autumn, when we could make up for lost time. Then I took my leave and went back to call for Rilke.

He looked much better and was calm, almost cheerful, as so often after a violent attack. He was waiting for me on the terrace of the hotel and came across to my gondola. Again, as we set out happily together, I felt that the past few days had been nothing but an evil dream. He did not want to go by water. "It is so much better to walk beside the little canals. You see many beautiful old houses and all the little bridges, sometimes roofed-in, and ancient shops on quiet squares."

It was a delicious outing. We saw the Campo Morosini and the sunny church of San Stefano with the adjoining cloister, where unfortunately one can hardly recognise what remains of Pordenone's magnificent frescoes. We saw the wonderful Palazzo Pisani with its spacious chambers and splendid interior decoration, and we saw the high altar in the church of San Vitale. We passed through many narrow streets beside the lesser canals, over bridges and by discreet little stone-walled gardens. Then we came back to the Campo Sant' Angelo and went by way of more narrow bridges and lanes to the Palazzo Contarini with its entrancing *Scala a chiocciola,* a magical spiral stairway in a slender tower of shining marble. Finally, on our way back, we

came to St. Maria del Giglio. Through the main doorway we
heard singing. The door was closed only by a curtain and, as we
went in, a short Capuchin father mounted the pulpit and began
to preach. His good-natured, rosy, boyish face was framed in a
long black beard which gave him an air of comic dignity like a
dressed-up child. He began to speak in a thin, high voice,
having first silenced with a reproachful look two children who
were throwing dice behind a side altar.

I had heard from Rilke that religion in Italy is, so to speak, a
family matter, and now I saw it for myself. Women of all ages,
including young mothers, who were not above changing their
infants' napkins in the corner of a pew, listened attentively to the
words of the little priest, as he spoke of the training of children
and exhorted them not to be too lenient. He dealt particularly
with the problem of cinemas and worked himself into a genuine
Italian passion as he dwelt on the dangers that might befall the
ragazze and *figliuoli*, if they were allowed to enter these dens of
iniquity. He spoke the most delightful Tuscan dialect and his
Venetian listeners probably hardly understood him. He became
so heated that he raised his hands to heaven and cried to the
women in a growing crescendo: "When the children come and
beg their mothers, 'Mamma, mammina, let me go to the
cinema,' what will a good mother answer?"

He paused and looked expectantly at his hearers. They smiled
back at him fearlessly or curiously, as though to say: Well,
fratello, tell us—what is a good mother to say when the children
come and ask to be allowed to go to the cinema?

Yes, he knew the answer and let them have it: "A good
mother says: No, no, no!"

He did not speak these three negatives, he *sang* them with all
the warmth of his conviction, as though he could thus snatch the
bambini from the clutches of the film-devil. Then the sermon was
finished, the women murmured "*grazie*" and hurried cheerfully
into the open air with their children.

As we got into a gondola we saw the identical mothers and
children crowding round the box-office of a cinema, where
coloured posters advertised a truly hair-raising film. Rilke could not
help smiling. "The poor little father was no match for the devil!"

Then we went to call on Princess Marie, who was very glad to
welcome "our Serafico".

(From the Diary.)

Baron Franchetti has kept his word and invited us to inspect his art-treasures. It is delightful to enter a *palazzo* as a guest, without first having to deal with the numerous strangers, door-keepers and guides.

The party consisted of Princess Marie, her cousin, Rilke and myself. The baron welcomed us in the charming courtyard of the *Ca' d'oro*, by an open marble staircase, supported by three Gothic arches, which ascends lightly and airily to the doorway on the first floor. In the courtyard are palms and other fine plants in barrels; the slender columns of the open hall that surrounds two sides of the yard are covered with delicate creepers, while the entire opposite wall is overgrown with dark-green ivy.

I inquired about the origin of the name *Ca' d'oro*, and the baron explained that the ornaments on the façade were gilded when Matteo Roverti and the two Buons completed the palace for a Contarini in 1436. The name, "the Golden House" was retained, though the brilliance of the ornamentation paled with the centuries. Later there were changes of ownership, the palace fell into decay, the pictures were not restored, the precious reredos in the chapel, a St. Sebastian by Montegna, was coated with the yellow wax of flickering candles.

Franchetti has made it his life's work to restore the *Ca' d'oro* to its original splendour. Rilke says that explains why the baron lives so modestly and frugally. He does not even allow himself a servant, and his personal accommodation is confined to two little rooms under the roof. After greeting us he invited us to tea in his "monastic cell", and afterwards to a tour of the palace. "Unless we do it in that order," he said, in a tone of apology, "you would think my apartments more primitive still."

His sitting-room was very simply furnished, but had a wonderful view of the *canal grande*. A round table was laid with a yellow damask cloth and very valuable old porcelain, and a camellia, covered with bloom, stood in a chased bronze vessel in the middle of the room. The princess was right: this "last aristocrat of Venice" could afford to dispense with a crowd of liveried servants, and to prepare the tea with his own hands on a little electric cooker and hand it round with the sandwiches. "He has the best recipe for spinach and parmigiano sandwiches," revealed the princess. "Caterina, who cooks for him, does not understand such specialities, although she makes the best *pasta reale* in the world. But she learnt that from our Giglia in Sagrado, didn't she, Baron?"

After tea, Franchetti took us to the chapel to see the Mantegna, which is shortly to be cleaned and restored under the supervision of a specialist. Unfortunately no one will be able to get a proper impression of this glorious painting until the restoration is completed. Rilke inquired about a van der Goes, which used to hang in one of the smaller rooms, but we could not see the Dutch paintings; they have all been sent to the *Accademia* to be cleaned. Franchetti showed us many other family treasures, however, a Venus of Titian, an Annunciation by Carpaccio, Venetian subjects by Guardi, and paintings by Signorelli, Botticelli, Tullio Lombardi and other artists whose names I have unfortunately forgotten. The most valuable pictures in the collection are said to be several portraits by Tintoretto, which the baron showed us with exceptional love and pride. There is wonderful furniture too in all the rooms. It is to be arranged to form a complete reproduction of a rich fifteenth-century Venetian house. The baron intends later on to open the *palazzo* to the public as a museum and to bequeath it to the city of Venice, "as a slight acknowledgment of my good fortune in having been born here and allowed to live here." He also showed us the spot at the foot of the lovely staircase in the courtyard where one day he will be buried.

I felt quite moved as I took leave of this extraordinary man, and I bore away with me a glowing memory of the afternoon we had spent with him. Rilke is very fond of him, too, and the three of us talked at length of this unusual personality as we made our way home.

There were many more hours in which everything seemed gay, light and untroubled, though we had not yet discussed and clarified the parting that lay before us. Should we meet again? And what would that meeting be like? Our minds were full of these questions and decisions, but we forgot them in those moments when we understood each other with our very souls and grasped each other's being completely.

Once more the inner light flamed up. Wondering and, as it

were, bewitched, we walked about Venice, that shimmering dream of marble and water, and when we spoke to each other it was as Rainer had once said: ". . . did I ever speak to anyone before you were here? No, Benvenuta, no! I do not know by what means I communicated myself to others. I just went at it, I believe I simply overran them all—and then they lay around and were dead, or they stepped aside in alarm at the last moment and I rushed on round the world like a blind man, still thinking I was moving round inside people (God knows why). To speak to you is not to act outwards, but to go within; it is to grow a little where no one sees, as a child stirs in its mother's womb . . ."

Later, many years later, looking back on this unforgettable and agonising period, I felt that the days in Venice before we parted contained so much that was mild and gentle because each of us was trying to make things smooth for the other before the inevitable separation, to avoid awakening the pain that still lay in the future. It was like a warm, sunny day before the onset of winter, when all the flowers bloom afresh, all the colours sparkle in earth and sky for a last time before the snow wipes them out.

And, since that was our feeling, we wanted to tell each other how beautiful was life's Yes, and when we spoke of something grave or sad, we were imbued with the will to propitiate, to accept and bear it, like the monk in the Indian legend who contemplated life without desire or denial. For we knew this too: if we should meet again we should be different; it would be like reunion after resurrection, all pain having been overcome in an earlier life, the burning grief having been stilled by time.

(From the Diary.)

Rilke has been telling me about Duse, whom he first met here in Venice. He was a young man, she a prematurely ageing woman, who had passed the zenith of life and fame and seemed to be without future. He had seen her many times on the stage and had long wished to meet her. "For years and years I had longed to meet her without doing the slightest thing to bring it about. Now it came a thousandfold, not *one* meeting, many, daily, at her place and at mine, with Venice as the background. I lived deep inside it, as in a fairy tale. Lived?—Suffered, suffered! O Benvenuta, it was this that drove the breach through my whole inner nature, so that if one thing in all these years reached fulfilment, grandly, nobly, unstintingly, it was still like that velvet cushion in the Thermal Museum at Rome, which bears the head of the 'dying Gaul'—a fine, soft support for a still uncomprehended, irrevocable woe.

"Duse often came to see me. She lived quite near. Her gondola would suddenly turn out of the lagoon into my canal and I could recognise her as I sat at my writing-desk. So we saw each other. I do not know whether our impulse was somehow to help each other, but we each had in us so much that was malign that when we piled it in layers we stood finally aloft in a clear but lifeless air, as on a pyre heaped day and night, and, although we never put it into words, we could fancy that God finally set fire to this dry and woeful structure and it consumed both us and Him . . ."

There was a garden which Duse had often visited with Rilke. He asked if he might take me there, for it was a fantastic garden with meadows and mown hay, like the parks of the north, but also with vines, oleanders, laurels and cypresses.

We took a gondola and threaded our way through a maze of small canals to a part of the city I had never seen before. There were almost no footpaths; the steps outside the quiet palaces led straight to the water and could be reached only by boat. Sometimes we saw a tree-top rising above and behind the locked door of a little garden. Ivy and caper-bushes sprawled over the grey stones. At last we came to a flight of steps that led to a high gateway, in which was a locked postern. The gondolier pulled the bell-rope, a bell tinkled, someone opened a spy-hole and inquired who was there. Rilke passed his card in and we heard footsteps retreating. Rilke said that the *giardino Eden* was now the property of an eccentric old Englishman, who never showed himself but gave admission to the few strangers who knew of his garden and sent in a visiting card. The postern opened and we entered a southern paradise. A path ran between tall vines to a group of olive and fig trees; beyond was a curved path formed of bowers of roses and ending in a parterre of lovely flower beds. A stone balustrade ran along the edge of the sea, enclosing a spacious meadow. The grass had been mown and haycocks were dotted among the cypresses, whose tips stood out black against the deep-blue sky.

I could understand why Duse's restless heart had sought peace in this wondrous garden. Sunshine lay over the water; there was hardly a ripple to be seen; the sea was sleeping, an azure mirror, like that which spread before the bench where we had often sat at Duino. Here too there was a seat straight in front of us, beside the wall and next to a huge oleander bush. We sat down, looking across at the distant island of San Michele, where the dead of Venice had once been laid in their last resting-place.

Memories awoke. ". . . here in this garden I wrote a letter on Duse's behalf, urged on by the restless desire to keep some theatre open for her, in case she was still capable of acting again. I was plagued by her wish to act, 'une seul fois, bien armée, mais tranquille', as she put it. Think of it, the moment went by—it could only be a moment, worn out as she was—went by because the two or three people who could have arranged it negotiated instead of acting, because no one showed any energy and nothing was ready. I felt as though the dying Chopin were longing to play for the last time, to play his soul across, to guide it into eternity, while those around him were disputing as to whether there was a piano, whether they could bring it up to his room and —how much it would cost! I *could* not bring myself to believe that she would go down in sickness, misery, obscurity; she deserved, she demanded, a glorious end where she had so magnificently begun—on the stage. But it was too late!"

We walked back through the enchanted garden, where dusk was now falling. Only the houses and churches still shone on the distant islands, where the last sun-rays lingered as though unwilling to depart. Our gondola was waiting at the gate. The door closed behind us. Duse's garden vanished from our sight.

My mind keeps returning to the meeting of Duse and Rilke. Two great ones met, and the result was hopelessness, fear, depression. They sought to help each other, but there was "too much that was malign"!

I am full of deep feeling for such relationships, but it is not in my nature to understand them easily. I must learn completely to comprehend other people, and thank God He has given me what Rainer calls the "indestructible happiness of the soul". It is, I think, the courage to live and a belief in happiness; in times of stress one always fights one's way back to it, if only one has an affirming heart. Rainer knows better than anyone what is meant by an affirming heart, but he does not possess it. His heart has only a boundless comprehension of the inner motions of nature and of man. He has the gift of knowing what takes place invisibly behind phenomena, the gift of expressing the apparently inexpressible, till one contemplates the depth, the goodness, the purity of his noble mind as though it were a miracle. Yet this noble humanity of his is in itself the source of his dualism and his suffering. How moved I was once when he spoke of the "inadequacy" of his own nature. ". . . the saint engaged my attention so inexpressibly because he alone succeeds in forming neither floods nor marshes; he does not dry up, nor seep away through tiny runnels into the sand—he has nothing to do but collect all the pure channels of his heart, to gather up a hundred unconscious springs, in order, by the ever growing richness of his nature, to pour himself into God's stony river-bed, swirling, swirling with foreknowledge of the infinite estuary."

And he found words for what has lived within him, only half-conscious but formative for his whole life: "How I have longed to be like him. But have I not been born through my art more deeply into humanity—should I live apart from humanity and not know it? Not know it in its simple, guileless charity, in its assuagement, in its rich urgency?"

Rainer, dear, dear Rainer, have you forgotten those other sentences of yours, when, in a great and agonising hour, you tried to establish your life in humanity, and spoke the word "always"? Have you forgotten those other words?—"Whenever I was under an obligation to life or leagued myself with it, I could not; I withdrew myself I know not whither, I retracted everything." Have you forgotten?

But I will save you from retracting, and myself too, Fra Angelico: I will tell you to go when your ship is ready to carry you into distant seas of solitude, there where work has its "primeval claims" on you, more paramount claims than I could ever have. Thus today I have spoken to you in my heart and you do not know it. And you shall never learn how unutterably I suffer in this lonely hour, when I finally know that I will not— dare not—go with you!

What a good thing it is that there are people who know nothing about us, who do not divine the hours of suffering we have to endure, and live their own tranquil lives, happy and light-hearted.

It was pleasant to get to know Countess Valmarana and her daughter, a gentle, quiet, very lovable girl. It is in their house that the princess has her *mezzanino*—bedroom, living-room and a circular dining-room. In contrast to Duino everything is smaller and prettier. The *palazzo* has the same effect as a water-colour by Tiepolo. The rooms are not large, the furniture is half empire, half biedermeier—a clavecin, brightly-polished cup-boards and cabinets with gilded chocolate-cups and little, old Viennese figurines inside them, and some miniatures above the light, cherry-wood sofa with its dark blue silk cover striped with old rose.

The countess and her daughter came to tea with Princess Marie and brought with them an old abbé, their family priest. He is eighty years of age, a charming old man, still robust, with a fresh-coloured face and snow-white hair. In Italy girls are not allowed on the streets alone, so when the countess or her com-panion cannot go, the abbé accompanies the daughter in the gondola, goes shopping with her, takes her to a friend's house and fetches her again at the appointed hour. I feel that they are good, warm-hearted people. After tea we went up to their rooms. The countess asked me to play; she apologised for her piano, which, she said, was of a make probably unknown to me: would I like to try it first? Great was her astonishment when I found to my delight that it was an old Bösendorfer. I told her no other instrument was so dear and familiar to me as a member of that wonderful family. As I played, I rid my heart of much anxiety and sadness; I felt at ease and at home with these loving, sym-pathetic women, and when I took leave of them it was as though I were parting from old friends.

I have not seen Rainer today. He left early this morning by the first train for Padua. But tonight I found on my table a bunch of lovely dark-red roses with a little card, "*à demain!*" There are roses in my room every evening. How long will that go on? In a few days I shall leave to join Maria.

Now that I am alone again in the stillness of this great, antique room, I am afraid. Afraid of the end, afraid of myself, lest at the last moment I should turn back, terribly afraid of loneliness, without my beloved consoling voice, without Fra Angelico. And I feel a burning sense of longing. For what? For something strong, bright, powerful, for a high heart, unknown and far away, that will carry me into the safety and protection of an *undivided* world.

Rainer, Rainer, forgive me!

In these last days in Venice we have only once spoken of separation, when Rilke said he would go to Assisi. Then I called up all my courage; I did not flinch, even when I saw in his eyes a glimmer of the ultimate question. I said, with all the warmth I could summon, "I wish from the bottom of my heart that all your days there may be blessed with work and peace."

I thought I noticed that his face turned a shade paler, but he bowed and looked at me with infinite tenderness. "And you——?"

"I am going to Maria." My voice failed and I turned away to hide the hot tears that ran down my cheeks.

Then he was standing beside me, quiet and erect. He lifted my face towards him. "Don't be afraid, beloved child," he said softly but firmly. "Don't be afraid. I am going back to torments I have never escaped. Everything is as it must be. You are right, and that is good."

In the afternoon I went to take leave of the princess. She had sent a note, saying she wished to speak to me, "*mais toute seule, je vous en prie.*"

She received me with great earnestness. She was usually reserved in her attitude to other people's affairs, but she inquired about my immediate plans and what I intended to do in the future. I told her I should go first to my sister, then, after a fortnight's concert-tour, home to my parents. Later, I wanted to be alone somewhere with a piano and leisure to prepare myself for the coming winter, when I had to play at Hamburg, Leipzig, Königsberg, Riga, Warsaw and perhaps several places in Russia. She looked at me for a while, and said suddenly, "Do you know, you are much too good for a life like that? It is only flight, evasion, nothing but a succession of difficulties with agents, managers and such-like. You are so strong and vital; you have in you so great a capacity for making others happy, but—may an old woman say this who is very fond of you?—what you are doing now is not right for you."

I must have looked startled, for she went on to answer my

many unspoken questions: "You will bring your nature to its finest flower only when you can rest, *rest*, grow and develop in the love and strength of another. Someone should come and take you—not to suffering but to the light."

That was too much. Suddenly I was on my knees and my head was in her lap. Her arms were round me. "I know that it is terribly hard for you," she said, "but *he cannot*. You must realise that. He would like to, his heart burns with longing, and that only makes him still more wretched. You have great power over him—perhaps you do not know how much he loves you—but his dæmon also has great power. He wavers between you and the task he has to accomplish, and sometimes it seems to me that he is depressed and disappointed because you are a vital, independent personality, and not simply the will-less handmaid that—perhaps—he needs. He himself only half understands it and half puts it into words; half he clings to what your strength and vitality mean to him. With him it is Yes and No at the same time. It seems to me impossible for you two to live together permanently; there would be ceaseless inner conflict, in the course of which you would have to sacrifice all your gaiety for a life of pain and renunciation."

"And if I did it all the same?" I cried in despair.

"No," said the princess, "you will not do it. You must not, for you would destroy your own life and would still be unable to help him. His fate is to be alone; his sacrifice is pain. That lifts him up to great, new, creative work. But your destiny is the light. Do you understand me?"

She looked at me, full of love and sympathy.

"If you see our Serafico again at some later date, all will be clearer, calmer and lovelier than it is now."

I kissed her hand and she embraced me. "Good-bye, child," she said. "Think lovingly of our Duino and all the beautiful moments of these last few weeks."

The Countess Valmarana sent a message, asking to be allowed to come down for a moment, so I hastily withdrew. At the door, the princess offered me the use of her gondola; she did not need it again that day; I was to go out somewhere, and afterwards Prospero would bring me back to my hotel. I could hardly thank her. Almost out of my senses I went down the steps to the canal, where the gondola was waiting. I said something that Prospero did not understand; he repeated his question. "To the island of San Michele."

We passed out into the lagoon.

I shed no tears. I think everything inside me was turned to stone. I only wanted to be in some place where all was at rest— life and joy and pain.

The gondola slid noiselessly over the still water in the evening sunshine. Now I could make out distinctly the straight tops of the cypresses rising above the cemetery wall. I had an etching of Böcklin's "The Isle of the Dead", and had once written underneath it these words from Zarathustra: "This is the isle of graves, the silent isle; here too are the graves of my youth. I will take there an evergreen wreath of life."

It seemed to me that the picture had come to life and I was actually moving towards Böcklin's Isle of the Dead. But I had no wreath of life in my hands. All living things seemed far away; it was as though I could never be gay again, as though the words which a warm-hearted, motherly woman had spoken to me had brought everything permanently back into my mind with painful clarity, to brood there for ever like a shadow over my days.

". . . perhaps you do not know how much he loves you," the princess had said (oh, how well I knew it!) and, "you would still be unable to help him," and, "his sacrifice is pain." . . .

A girl was sitting outside the church selling decorations for the graves, poor little wreaths of cypress sprays decked with paper roses, china angels and candles in shallow clay vessels. I asked for a few flowers. I did not know why. To whose grave should I take them? The girl hurried away and, coming back, handed me a carnation plant. Then I passed through the gateway into the churchyard.

Many of the graves were old and dilapidated; others were covered with flowers. I read the names: Andrea Villati, Gemma Fontana, Ernesto Claricini—unknown men and women, unknown destinies, unknown woe. None of them wanted my flowers; I walked on past them, distraught and confused. They had others who remembered them or had grievously loved them; they did not need me. A mound, smothered in periwinkle, lay almost completely hidden at the end of an avenue. No one seemed to have been there for months. The inscription on the gravestone, once cut in letters of gold, was hardly legible: "Here lies my bride, who died on her wedding day. Girls, pray by her grave that her innocent soul may bless you and you may become as she was."

I put my carnation plant on this grave, knelt down before it and laid my face in the cool greenery.

". . . through pain to climb far out of life, and grow far out of time." Was it this that was laid upon me? Had one to grow out of life through suffering before one could return, indestructible, removed from all the confusions and errors and contradictions of youth?

And suddenly I knew: here before me, on the grave of this girl, the evergreen wreath of life was blooming in a hundred tiny blue flowers—and a mysterious power had led me here to see it. . . . And she, perhaps she was happy, united in some nameless bourne, to which we cannot attain, with him who had grieved for her.

I plucked a spray of periwinkle and took it away. Outside, the gondola was waiting. Dusk had fallen; the first stars flamed out as I left the gondola at the Corte Barozzi and went up the stairs to my room.

We were walking once more through Venice. It was our last day.

We talked calmly and composedly. It was as though all our feelings were frozen. As we crossed a bridge a file of gondolas came towards us, bearing a wedding-party. The bride in her white veil and chaplet of myrtle nodded happily to us and threw Rainer a flower from her bouquet. Children were playing in the Piazza St. Margherita. Outside the Museo Tiepolo we met Franchetti. He asked if I was coming to the reception of Mme. de Pourtalès on the following Monday. No, Rilke told him, I was leaving early next day. "What a pity!" cried the baron. "But if you once love Venice you always come back!" Then we went all three to St. Maria Formosa and stopped in front of the famous painting of St. Barbara. Franchetti explained where and when Palma Vecchio had painted it. Outside, by the Palazzo Querini, he left us. I saw and heard all this as though through a veil of mist; my comments and answers were almost automatic. Rilke hardly spoke.

In the afternoon he went to see the princess, who was returning to Duino. I sent her flowers with my warmest greetings and thanks. I felt it impossible to see her again in Rilke's presence. That evening I had a cup of tea and a snack in my room, wrote a few letters and sent a telegram to Maria. When Rilke came he told me there was a festival on the Grand Canal, and, looking out of the window, we saw decorated gondolas making their way towards the Piazzo San Marco. Expectant crowds lined the banks, waiting to enjoy the pretty sight. More and more gondolas arrived, till at last the canal was crowded with craft of all sizes. Coloured lanterns were lit, painted with flowers, butterflies, fish and birds.

And then the ancient verses of Tasso rang out, sung by the beautiful voices of the gondoliers on that warm, spring evening.

We sat in the alcove, full of sorrow and the pangs of parting, looking down on that gay scene, as though it were a glittering, bright, coloursome dream of a world that ebbed from us towards others who were gay and happy. We sat for a long time in silence; the decorated gondolas glided away, and at last the old palaces were quiet again in the moonlight.

Then Rilke began to speak. Once more, like a man taking leave for good, he spread out his whole life before me, his youth and all the years of quest and renunciation, all the joy of creation, all the trials of daily life, all the flights, the yearnings and the hours of peace. Truly the life of a great man, a fighter and a solitary, with all its truth and all its errors—and even they were worthy of respect because of their purity. He thanked me for the brightness I had brought to him, and said he believed that what he had been able to give me was the greatest and deepest he had ever written: his letters, the expression and testimony of his whole life.

He spoke of the wonderful beginnings of our time together, and of how much wretchedness he had brought, inevitably, into our happiness. "But my withered, sick nature has become more visible to me in the warm, strong light of your being, and now I must live on as before you came, except that I am the richer for this most bitter experience."

I thought: Can I, should I, go on living? Do I not owe a debt to my comforting voice, my saviour?

And then at last I could give utterance to all that was in my mind—my unbounded love, my deep gratitude, all my doubts and confusions, the conflicting voices within me of misery, renunciation, separation. And he understood, as he had always understood completely every motion and obligation of the human soul. He gathered my unrestrained confession into the goodness of his heart and, rising above it, succeeded in comforting me as none other could have done.

"All the same, everything is right," he said tenderly. "For one imperishable, eternal moment of God I was in the depths of your soul, of your heart, like a child in the mother. That knowledge we cannot lose, it can only mean a still deeper access to our own lives."

Outside, the dawn was breaking. The house-fronts awoke in a pale, frosty light; the first freight-barges passed on their way to market; we heard the boatmen call to each other, then all was still again.

"Come," said Rainer. "Rest a little. It is too late to go to bed. Close your eyes. I will tell you when it is time to wake." He saw that I was cold in my light frock, so he took my travelling rug and wrapped it round me. Then he put his arm about my shoulders and laid my head on his breast. I felt his hand gently stroking my eyes, then I fell asleep, tired to death.

When I awoke and sat up, the morning was bright with sunshine. Rilke was sitting there as before, his eyes fixed on me with an expression of quiet goodness. He said, "Forgive me, but I had to wake you or you would have been too late for your train. I will go now, and fetch you in an hour's time."

My head was aching and my limbs were quite stiff from sleeping in my clothes. I took a hot bath and drank a cup of steaming tea. When the hour had passed and Rilke came, I was waiting in hat and coat.

We shook hands again. For the first and last time we kissed each other with warm and tranquil devotion. It was like an unspoken prayer, and gave to our life together its final dedication. Then, without looking back, I went down the stairs.

The gondola was waiting outside. We set off into a sunny May morning, but my eyes were full of tears, and I saw nothing of the bright magic of that færy city.

The last thing I really saw was Rainer himself, standing outside the lowered window of the railway carriage, looking up at me. And in farewell I sank my whole feeling, my most ardent love—a warm, unspoken thanks—into his eyes, into his heart.

As the train began to move, I took in for the last time the slight, dark figure. With an abrupt movement he snatched at my hand. Then the scene dropped behind and I was alone.

War

WHEN I reached Bolzano, Carl and Maria were waiting for me at the station. My sister looked well and blooming again, and she embraced me with gentle anxiety. "You've got so thin! Now you must rest and let us thoroughly spoil you. And we have a surprise for you."

We drove down a hill, through an avenue of chestnuts, to a gay house with red-and-white shutters. As the horses stopped at the door, I saw a dear face smiling down at me: my father was standing on the top step with his arms held out to me. "Papa!" I cried, surprised and touched. I felt myself reel and someone catch and hold me. Then I lost consciousness.

"There now, she's opening her eyes," said a kind, cheerful voice and, as though just awakened from a deep dream, I saw a figure bending over my bed and the face of our old friend and physician, Dr. Christoforo. As though from a great distance, I heard him say, "Do you know, my dear, that you have slept like a log for three nights and two days?"

I tried to sit up but he pressed me gently back into the pillows. "Where are you?—You are at home. We carried you in from the carriage and put you in the guest room. You simply dropped down before our eyes. What's this?—Tears? That's a fine thing! Now you will eat a hearty meal and tomorrow you will get up. We will soon get your nerves right again."

"But how did you get here from Munich, Uncle?"

"I'm on holiday, my child. I'm staying three more days, then I must leave. Just long enough to get you on your feet again. After that you will be able to look after yourself."

I was at home. I could rest. They asked no questions but nursed me like a child. When I was able to get up, my father and Maria showed me over my sister's new home. It lay on the slope of a hill, surrounded by beautiful gardens. From the terrace one had a view of an open, smiling landscape. The whole valley lay at our feet and, with its chestnut woods, vineyards and the many villages, castles and ruins scattered on the opposite slopes and hills, it was like a gay fairy country, created in one of God's spendthrift moods.

Somewhere, as though far away, lay a heavy burden, but it no longer oppressed me. It was as Uncle Christoforo said: "When you feel as though you have lost much blood, mentally and physically light, almost floating, then you are over the hill."

The good, wholesome will to live awoke again. And one day I was able to ask Maria whether Rilke had written. She had not dared to tell me before, but now I learned that he had telegraphed his address and greetings from Assisi a short time before. Carl had written immediately to Professor Permacchi, director of the Franciscan library, whom he had known for some time, and asked him to give Rilke access—if he wished to work there—to the rare treasures of the library, which were not otherwise available. Now Rilke had sent his thanks, and added that he was returning to Paris in a day or two. It was a sad letter, as though written on a sultry day in some forgotten country. We read it in the garden under the bluest of South Tyrolean skies, while Mario played and chuckled near-by in his wicker perambulator.

"You are worlds apart," said Maria with a loving glance at her child. "Here everything is so good and peaceful—and there he is tormenting himself. Will it ever be otherwise with him? Do you know, I was very anxious about you, very anxious lest he should take you away from yourself. He is so wonderful, and yet I could be afraid of him." I put my hand on her arm. "Don't speak like that." But she hugged me with vehemence quite unusual and said, "We have you back, thank God! We have you back!"

(From the Lake Garda Diary.)

I have been living since the end of June in two little rooms in the Goethe House at Terbole. It is furnished with friendly, old-fashioned things that date from last century. I have a glorious view from the windows across the little harbour, which is full of the yellowish-red sails of fishing craft, and far to the south I can see the cliffs of Cape Campione. I have had a small piano sent from Riva. The days pass in a rhythm of work and leisure. My landladies—two sisters who have a dear old mother—are quiet and attentive and look after my daily needs. Sometimes toward evening Uncle Hans comes over from his olive-grove, where he is giving a course in painting, and brings the latest news into my solitude. To us here, in the peaceful sunshine, it seems quite incredible that some people really believe there may be a war.

Since papa was formerly an officer, he does not say much, but I can see from his letters that he is really expecting war to break out. Carl does not believe it. So opinions differ widely. Here everything is peaceful. The holiday-makers in the big hotel, Austrians and Germans, sit about on the shore or go sailing. Life goes on as usual. We are even preparing for a concert in aid of the family of a poor fisherman who is in trouble. Uncle Hans has painted a lovely poster. He will sing ballads by Löwe; a violinist and I are to play César Franck's sonata, then I shall play a cycle by Schumann and finally Schubert's Military March. A number of officers are coming over from the garrisons of Riva and Trient. We shall have a regimental band too, and, when the concert is over, it will play the national anthem on the big terrace of the hotel—a fine ending for the evening. I believe the young people are afterwards going to dance.

Among all these preparations an uneasy and anxious feeling sometimes overtakes me. What will the next few weeks bring with them? War, even the remote possibility of war, seems quite monstrous. Some people think that a war with the weapons of today could not last long, for everything would be destroyed, friend and foe, town and countryside.

At such times Rainer is a blessed help, even though from a distance. The weight of oppression between us is gone, and I think of the sweet and happy times we had together—they are nearer to me than anything else. In my *Book of Hours*[1] is a little dry twig from a wild rose. Rilke once took it out of his Spanish diary and gave it me, for it has a strange, individual scent, different from our hedge-roses.

"All the warmth of the sun is in it, and the southern country made it bloom more blissfully than its northern sisters," said Rainer. How deeply he had looked at Spain! How subtly he had felt the spring there!

". . . there, where one is aware of the sun throughout the winter, not merely as an object, but of its scarcely diminished

[1] Rilke's *"Stundenbuch"*.

effects, one feels not so much the inevitable joy that will come; one even watches without too great pleasure the progress of a few small almond-trees and the growing ostentation of the heavens; but let a warm cloudy day come unexpectedly—hark, how from early morn there is one feeling *more* in the noise of the birds, how it has grown darker, stands out almost with earnestness, purely sketched on the soft stillness. Go out: the greyness rests on your eye almost with the indulgence you feel from the inside of your lids, almost like sleep. And now too the more lavish pink of the trees becomes a miracle overnight, for it is *strong* in contrast with the lustrelessness of the unshed rain, strong with joy (not at all extravagant); and now place yourself so that it has the earth for background. Look, our earth, the heavy, cultivated, toilsome earth: it is still strong, the pink, but differently, as one is strong when one refuses to weep . . ."

In his last letter he wrote that he would try to work at the elegies again. It is a faint hope but even that is a blessing to him. How much I should like to tell him so, but I have to respect his solitude as sacred. I do not think he will leave now; he will probably stay in Paris for the summer, for his health seems better, thank heaven. "I am generally at home, very quiet, very lonely, but otherwise well," he wrote. And I shall not answer him now. He does not even know where I am.

"His sacrifice is pain," said Princess Marie in that desperate hour in Venice. Now at last I fully understand his own words about sacrifice: "What is sacrifice? I believe it is nothing else than a person's unbounded resolve, no longer limitable in any direction, to achieve his purest inward potentiality." A sentence read at random in a periodical had aroused this conviction in him, but had also dismayed him and, as it were, rent him asunder. ". . . the bad, diluted, Christian use of the term had made it suspect to me—and what it may actually have been in its fiery, antique meaning no one has yet really revealed to our minds. But now, there it was—'The way from talent to greatness is through sacrifice'. . . . It struck right through me. Like a dagger sharpened for use against me, which the assassin had carried a whole year under his cloak, always in his ready hand—it struck into me as such a dagger suddenly leaps out and into the solid breast. Yes, there it was: I had the talent, I had it in high degree, but I had nothing else. If my work was to stand, the other thing was needed—greatness. Here suddenly the bridge was given a name: where is my sacrifice?"

Does he know now where it is? And are its blessings also given to him? He believes in higher powers within us and above us and raises his hands to realms higher than the earthly—therein lies his overwhelming power, his influence on others. There is a certainty in him that in daily life has become a burden. He, for whom the slightest reference to the world around is often an effort, could once utter the proud sentences that apply unerringly to his own life: "When I saw that the others strained toward God, I could not understand; for although perhaps I had less of Him than they, yet there was no one in the way between us and I was easily brought to His heart. For it is for Him to take us; our part is hardly more than to be within His reach."

Once when we had read the letters of St. Augustine together, we discussed the question of how hard men must struggle to reach their highest wisdom, the "peace in God". Rilke expressed the opinion that Meister Eckhart had always appeared to him the most wonderful figure of the early Middle Ages with his purest relation to the highest, for "in the sound substance of the soul there is no effort toward God. Love to God was the quiet, predominant direction of his nature." I see with increasing clearness that Rilke must give up longing for his own life to make contact with humanity in order that he may rest completely in the sphere of the divine.

How sad it is to think that Rainer does not like this wonderful landscape round Lake Garda. He once said that it is connected with too many memories of his mother, of her "spectrally false and forced goodness to me". He said this, although no one can speak like him of the deepest essence of mother-love. He needed the love of a real mother as he needed air to breathe, and could have unfolded his shy child-life in it. And, as though he had harboured and developed inside him all his life the yearning to express such a love, he could sometimes be almost as delicate of feeling as a woman, giving to others what he himself had so bitterly lacked.

I remember once in Paris he came up to my room and found me in a state of fear and alarm. That morning a letter had arrived, an evil and menacing echo from the past, and although it could not harm me any more, I was so completely overcome with horror that I was almost out of my senses and had an intolerable headache. I sat in an arm-chair by the window, crying. Rainer asked no questions; he put his hand on my eyes. "Dear, you will grow calm again," he said. "It is nothing. What could happen to you?" His kind, loving voice went on speaking. It was as though a marvellous peace came over me. Then I fell asleep. When I awoke life was joyous again and the pain had gone. Thus the protective calm of his heart, that could find no peace for itself, could bring peace to others.

I think of all that as I sit on the shore in the evening reading *Malte*.

The people here are very nervous and are asking themselves what the next few days will bring forth. Perhaps we shall hear something more definite from the officers who are coming to the concert the day after tomorrow. I shall write to Rainer, but he, no doubt, is safe in Paris, thank God! All the same, I should like to know exactly where he is.

What terrible days we have been through!

We had our concert in the lounge of the Grand Hotel. It was full of festive people, men in uniform, well-dressed women, many young girls. Uncle Hans sang splendidly; there was loud applause, bunches of flowers and—most important—a large contribution for the poor children of the fisherman.

When the concert was over the folding doors that give on the terrace were opened. The regimental band from Riva had taken up its position outside. The conductor raised his baton—but before the first notes of Haydn's fine old national hymn could ring out, a door was thrown open and a clear, shrill voice shouted "War!"

What happened next can hardly be described. The word was hurled like a trumpet-tone into a room full of people who, a moment before, had been happy and gay. An indescribable tumult broke out. The men rushed to the telephone and it was besieged in a moment. The orderly who had brought the news was immediately surrounded. People were shouting for their cars and carriages. The women, helpless and distracted, could not understand that a gust of enthusiasm had swept through the place. There were tears and laughter. Officers shook each other's hands, shouting, "At last! Thank God! At last!" Then everyone rushed out. In a few minutes the great lounge was empty. For a time I heard agitated voices outside, then the hooting of cars and the clatter of horses' hoofs from departing carriages.

The wall-lamps and crystal candelabra filled the empty lounge with light. Uncle Hans and I were suddenly standing alone in a deathly silence, looking at each other. We could not speak. We walked back to the vestibule, between overturned chairs and white programmes, lying crushed on the floor, while an old servant, trembling and quite distracted, began to put out the lights.

There was a crowd around the hotel-desk. People were inquiring excitedly about communications and train connections. Trunks were being taken up in the lifts. It seemed as though everyone was in flight.

In the street people were standing together in groups, the men grim, the women shy and tearful. It was as though the sky had suddenly fallen. Uncle Hans took me home and promised to come back first thing in the morning: perhaps by that time some details would be known.

My landladies were waiting for me in the Goethe House. Signorina Diomira helped me to change my clothes. "God in heaven! What will happen now?" she kept repeating. As I hung my glistening, silvery evening gown in the wardrobe, I felt I were discarding superfluous finery, and was suddenly ashamed of it.

"Signorina, is the post-office still open?" I asked foolishly. "Heavens!" she answered. "It is nearly midnight. Everything shuts at seven. Camillo has been here and told us he has to leave. An old man will take over his work at the post-office. God help us all!" Diomira wept.

We slept but little that night. The wind swept across the lake from the north in violent gusts, driving the waves before it. Lightning flashed somewhere; faint thunder rolled across the mountains. All night people stood in the streets, in groups, in pairs; once there was a loud sobbing. Morning came at last, a beautiful, bright morning. The landscape lay there as carefree and smiling in the summer sunshine as though there were no such thing as sorrow.

When I went to the post-office and tried to send a telegram to Rilke, Camillo told me the French frontier was closed. I was frightened to death and at first refused to believe it. Uncle Hans came at midday—he had been to Riva to hear the news—and told me we were at war with France too. My greatest anxiety is whether Rainer knows of all these dangers. It is a terrible thought that he may have been unaware of them and remained in Paris. He often goes for days without reading a newspaper or speaking to anyone, and then he hardly knows what is happening in the world. His last letter speaks of summer. ". . . I hope that with you too the year is keeping its promises. If only you could see the trees here: the recent, excessive heat has, as it were, parboiled them and taken half their leaves; something like an artificial October has resulted, and even the booths for the 14th July, which are going up at the entrance to the Luxembourg, are only a poor comfort for this."

Not a word of all that had been disturbing men's minds for weeks. On the contrary, he was delighted in his solitude to have received a probably rather crazy letter from Walter Heymel, the writer. Before we left Paris I had described to him an encounter I had had with Heymel in Merano, and he now wrote: ". . . the surprise you expressed about him makes me realise that, in recovering from his serious illness, he has remained just the same as of old. One never knew about him whether nature had made a whirlwind where he is or whether he incessantly produces out of himself this roar and whirl. And yet there is in all his utterances (not excepting the poems) a likable inability to act otherwise. As soon as one thinks of withdrawing from this commotion, as from a violent draught, it turns out to be a real wind, and one ends by feeling glad to be so delightfully out of doors . . ."

In these few words the whole essence of that strange man, Walter Heymel, seems to be comprehensively perceived and expressed. The letter was written about three weeks ago. It is calmer and gayer than the preceding letters, and with it came a very welcome gift—the copy of a poem I had asked for. But perhaps Rilke had known a few days later of the rumours that made the world hold its breath and had got away in time to Germany or Switzerland. Whom could I ask? They say Princess Marie has gone away; Titi Taxis knows nothing. This uncertainty is terrible! If only I could send him a message! If only I could warn him!

If I close my eyes I can see his two rooms in the rue Campagne première, the big studio and the little room adjoining. How often I have sat at Rodin's desk when Rilke was reading! Once he told me of Mont St. Michel, the dream-island in the sea. His eyes grew large and bright and we made plans to go there. He did not tire of describing the cathedral, that miracle of stone soaring into the sky, that concrete fervour of flaming faith and yearning for God. How near everything was—the countryside, art—to our humanity! And now?—"The French frontier is closed." And where is Rainer? Where is Rainer?

I left Terbole on the 13th August, 1914. I had been told that the railways would be closed for civilian passengers, perhaps for weeks, on account of the many military trains. At that time only one train still ran daily from the Tyrol to Upper Austria. I dared not delay.

I had packed my things and ordered a carriage for half-past two in the morning. I had to drive over the mountains to Mori to catch the train at half-past four. My dear landladies took leave of me with tears and blessings. Uncle Hans, who had always a word of reassurance, was grave and rather anxious because I was travelling alone. He could not get away himself, but I assured him that I was not in the least afraid. When we had left the village behind however and were driving up towards Nago, I felt a little alarmed at travelling alone with a strange coachman across the mountains and through the profound and spectral silence of the landscape.

There was a full moon and the night was of indescribable beauty. The lonely white road gleamed far ahead; now and then a soldier stepped out of the shadow of a rock, approached the carriage with fixed bayonet and stopped the horses. The driver had to show his permit, then we drove on. In the barren, rocky district of Loppio the few poor cottages were fast asleep, and I could not make out the little lake that must have been yonder in the sharp blue-black shadows of the cliffs. Only the strange church shone white in the moonlight, standing alone in the landscape like a Greek temple with pillared portico among the broken rocks and meagre grass.

It was as if one were driving on another planet. Only the warm odour of the two brown horses and their gentle snortings were soothing, earthy and comforting. Then we went steeply up-hill; lights shone in the distance—the railway-bridge at Mori. Suddenly we were in the midst of an indescribable chaos of locomotives, smoke, people, refugee trains, endless chains of trucks, singing soldiers, weeping women and frightened children.

And high above this human turmoil and these human destinies, high up in the mountains, came the dawn. The stars sank in a sky growing ever brighter; rosy pencils of cloud stood above the rocky peaks. This inexpressible peace in the awakening of nature was like a symbol of some higher being above our earthly affairs.

After a journey of twenty hours I arrived at last at Innsbruck, dead tired, and with little hope of finding Carl in the crowded station. But I saw him standing there on the platform, so tall that he towered above the rest. He took me to the Hotel Tirolerhof, where the bathroom had been requisitioned for me and made fit to live in. The town was overcrowded, the streets jammed with men and vehicles.

After I had rested a little, we sat till late in the little smoke-room of the hotel, where we were alone. Everyone had gathered in the dining-rooms and there was much singing and shouting there. This boisterous enthusiasm had something feverish about it. Carl, calm and collected as ever, brought greetings from Maria and spoke of her with great love and admiration. She had immediately taken over the management of the estate and was carrying on with exemplary prudence and common-sense. One or two trusty helpers were with her, but she had solid support from another quarter: some of Carl's family had escaped at great peril from Paris and after unspeakable difficulties reached Bolzano, where they had found shelter with Maria. They had had to leave everything behind but a small case, which they had carried with them.

Escaped from Paris! Carl said, as though he had guessed my thought, "By the way, do you know where Rilke is?" When I said No, he suggested that the safest thing would be to telegraph to Rilke's physician in Munich, Dr. von Stauffenberg. If Rilke was in Germany, Stauffenberg must know of it. Thank God we had found a way! In spite of the late hour, dear, good Carl sent an orderly to the station with my telegram. Carl was to leave next morning for the eastern frontier, where he would be exposed to a hard, uncertain fate. It was wonderful to feel his strength and confidence. He said he knew he would come back. "God grant it!" I thought with a fervent prayer. Maria's life was bound up inextricably with his—what would happen if he did not come back? When we took leave of each other, I thanked him from the bottom of my heart for all his brotherly love and loyalty. Then we parted: I went on with the next train and reached my destination—Gmunden on the Traunsee—after a journey of forty-eight hours.

(From the Diary.)

The journey from Innsbruck to Gmunden, which in peace-time occupies seven hours, took me two days and two nights. Never shall I forget that ghastly trip. The compartments were overcrowded; many people were travelling with children, who were the chief sufferers from the hardships of the journey, for sleep was impossible in the narrow compartments and there was no food to be had anywhere. Once, at a little station, people brought round coffee in tin wash-basins and stale bread that must have been many days old. It seemed as though everyone had lost his head.

I gave my small supply of chocolate and a packet of biscuits to two little girls, who were crying with hunger. The train stood still for one whole night in open country, while troop-trains steamed past one after the other. The waning moon hung in a clear sky and was reflected in the window-panes of the passing trains. The hot, stuffy air in our narrow compartment was unbearable. Now and then the guard came past. To the despairing question, "When shall we go on?" he answered always, "Some time."

It is infinitely soothing to be back here in our clean, quiet country house on the hill, and to be able to sleep again. But there is no news from Munich. Perhaps Stauffenberg has gone to some far-away hospital and cannot be reached. I have written to Elizabeth. Someone must surely know where Rilke is.

Today, when I came up from the lake, a white envelope was

lying on my table—a letter from Rainer! It seemed so incredible to see his writing again that at first I could not understand how he could have written. Yes, and there was a telegram too! Then I was holding the letter in my trembling hands.

"I feel it, dear, not without shame: you have been anxious about me and I have not hastened to reassure you, though I could have done so, for I was allowed to read your dear letter to Elizabeth. But will you believe me when I say that with all these incalculable events I have completely lost my writing-voice? Who *is*, who hears himself live and think and be? Am I still myself? I sometimes ask. Are we still ourselves?—No, we have all been born by force into an unheard-of world that has nothing in common with the world we knew before, except its incomprehensibility, but it is incomprehensible in a new, terrible, deadly way.

"None the less I have so far exactly carried out my previous plans: on the 19th July I left Paris with enough luggage for about two months; all the rest of my belongings remain there behind the locked door. I do not think of what may have become of them since, nor of whether they are lost for good.

"I went through Göttingen to Leipzig; thence on the 1st August to Munich, where I was treated by Stauffenberg (physically, not psycho-analytically). Yielding to his wishes, I moved about ten days ago into the country, but I see already that my stay will not last long or be of much advantage to me. How unattainable lies unsuspecting nature around us, just picture; the din of the times drowns and overwhelms all things.

"So I think it probable that I shall soon return to Munich and face the attempt to work, until such time as it becomes clear *how* I could merge my strength into the general sum of achievement. For the present I have too little to attack anything close at hand; if I could work my conscience would be clear. For only in my work do I serve truly and fully, and if it does not look like help at first glance, those who come back will some day want to make contact again with their earlier heart, and will be glad to find it continued, and to engage in the quiet domesticity of the spirit.

"But who thinks so far ahead? Today's happenings stand there like a vast perilous mountain-chain and the future of us all lies beyond and seems unattainable. The tension that I felt so strongly in Paris must therefore drive the whole world to a devastating discharge.

"God help me to find my way and to discover a place where I can be awake and sentient and capable even now of bringing forth from my heart the utmost and purest.

"My deepest greetings to you, dear. Your generous nature will, I know, itself support you and help you to be active and cheerful under the greatest trials, and to do good wherever you are . . ."

This letter had been written in the Landhaus Irschenhausen and had reached me in two days. Dr. Stauffenberg's telegram had taken eight days and bore the official stamp of several censors. Its contents were long out of date, for I had Rainer's letter in my hands, his heavy, dark and yet comforting letter, for he was alive, he had escaped all dangers and—best of all!—he wanted to work and seemed again completely to understand what work meant to him. ". . . for only in my work do I serve truly and fully . . ."

At the beginning of October we moved back into the town and I at once volunteered to organise concerts for the wounded in hospital. Letters came from various places with proposals, inquiries and glad approval. Professor Ludwig Schleich asked for a few evening concerts in Berlin; Leipzig inquired; so did Dresden, Königsberg, Hanover and Vienna. My friend Elizabeth, matron of a hospital in Munich, wrote asking me to come soon and play to her wounded. She said she had tried to persuade Rilke to come too, but he would probably be away for some time, moreover he did not feel capable at present of speaking before a large audience. She found him calm and composed but much changed; the war had no doubt affected him, or behind him lay trials from which he had not yet fully recovered.

With painful and anxious thoughts I set out on the 24th October for Munich, and although I told myself it would be much better not to see Rilke, the town seemed bare and deserted without him. All the sweet recollections of our stay on the way to Paris revived again and made the present seem pale and unreal.

I had informed a concert agency of my arrival. Next day, an agent got in touch with me just after lunch, visited me in my pension and brought with him a sheaf of proposals. I did not know him; he had an unpleasantly familiar way of speaking which aroused a sense of repulsion in me. I refused his offers and tried to terminate our conversation. He became importunate, then insolent, so I got up and went towards the bell by the door to call someone. The man made a movement as though to intervene— at that moment there was a knock, I cried "Come in," the door opened and Rilke was standing there!

I stared at him as though he were an apparition; the stranger vanished like a malevolent shadow and Fra Angelico and I were holding hands.

With one glance he had taken in the situation. After our first joyous greeting, I asked, still full of confusion, surprise and gratitude, how it had happened that he had arrived, a real guardian angel, just at that moment. He smiled a little and said simply, "That is what I am for."

I looked into his face, into his eyes, that shone clear and calm, and there came to my mind what I had so often thought in those troubled days in Venice: "If we should meet again we should be different; it would be like reunion after resurrection, all pain having been overcome in an earlier life, the burning grief having been stilled by time."

A quietude seemed to have entered into him. During the days, the beautiful, peaceful days, that followed, a kind of untroubled affection seemed to flower between us, like that of brother and sister; it made us happy and sometimes helped us to bear more easily the burden of the happenings in the world outside. We would not and could not speak of the future, that "lay beyond and seemed unattainable", but we could talk of all that was beautiful in our common memories, and we did so on long saunters through the English Garden, which, in these late autumn days, was still resplendent with green lawns and bright foliage. Often, at midday, we sat on a seat in the sunshine, watching the rapid, silent waters of the little streams glide past and enjoying the games of children and dogs, playing there on the paths without forebodings.

Once Rilke saved a little fox-terrier that had fallen out with several bigger dogs and could not defend itself against their attack. It was bowled right over, fell into the basin of a fountain, got its forepaws into the grating of the drain and began to whine piteously. Without stopping to think, Rilke stepped into the

water up to his knees and pulled the little dog out. In a joyous
dance of relief and freedom the little animal shook a shower of
water from its coat and began to roll in the grass. We could not
help laughing, but Rilke's shoes, his new blue suit, which, he
insisted, he had had made in my honour, and his grey cloth spats
were soaked through and through. Afraid lest he should catch
cold, I invited him to my room; we ran the few paces to the
pension and, while I made tea, he went to the bathroom and put
on a pair of stout woollen socks and leather slippers—much too
large for him—which I had bought to send to Carl at the front.

We were often light-hearted then. It was as if what Rilke had
written to me at Gmunden in the late summer was to prove
inevitably true even in daily life: ". . . those who come back
will some day want to make contact again with their earlier heart
and will be glad to find it continued. . . ."

Was the warm cheerfulness of the spirit also to be continued
by us, who were so closely bound by a common fate with all
those men, known and unknown, out there at the front?

I asked this question of Rainer and he answered that it was a
comfort too if positive life in its greatest and smallest mani-
festations remained indestructible. I admired the composure
with which he bore the happenings of the time; he seemed to face
life more calmly than ever before. He said nothing of his own
work and I did not dare to ask, but he often read aloud to me and
spoke of Goethe. He said he seemed to have discovered Goethe
only a few years before. ". . . formerly I had no real inclination
towards him . . . but now he is becoming significant to me, yes,
even humanly moving, for which I was least of all prepared. And
I constantly admire the magnificence and control with which he
went on building himself up on his foundations, restricting
himself at the top only because that was the spirit of his pyramid,
which he completed in symmetry . . ."

"Humanly moving!" I had never thought of Goethe like that,
but with Rilke's words the idea came to me with a new and
wondrous significance. By his power of feeling his way far into
the unique quality of a life, of a character, Rilke could bring close
to me the lives of strangers of whom I knew little. Thus his
admiration for Tycho Brahe, the great astronomer, was full of
wonder and delighted appreciation for this—to him—strange

M

science of the profound mysteries of the skies. And how cheerfully in all this he could regard himself as a "pupil" and
acknowledge himself to be wrong. ". . . it is simply lack of
talent: here I am living under this sky and when, as today, I wake
at dawn and the moon is standing in the centre of my south
window (and, by the way, it looked ill and neglected and passed
at once, high as it was, into the murk), I think it must have
made a mistake, for it seems so wrong of it to be just there. I said
to it, 'But my dear fellow——' and then it was gone. Its conscience cannot have been quite clear, and yet it was right of
course. Then I think of Tycho Brahe. At seventeen he left his
noble Danish kin and went to Leipzig to study law; he took a
few steps in that direction, but of nights (and Leipzig nights are
not exactly of the finest quality) he hung out of his little window,
while his tutor was asleep, and imprinted the bright sky on a ball
no bigger than his fist, one that could be conveniently hidden—
the night sky—got it, so to speak, dictated to his insight in the
most accurate order, one might almost say in rotation; his soul
sang it from the score at first sight (that is genius, dear). And
then a year later, walking slowly home one evening on the estate
of his Uncle Bille, he beheld with the naked eye the new star in
Cassiopeia—so familiar to him was that multitudinous dome that
the noiseless and minute addition became visible to his eye, as a
teacher sees one day that a shy new boy is sitting with the others
in his class.

"And I—I am stupidly surprised at the moon and suspect
something disorderly in its celestial behaviour. So the world
varies greatly in its closeness to us. I do not wish to calculate it
and spy it out and trick it into revealing its secrets, no, only to
enter everywhere into its laws by contemplation and joy, for that
way is easy and there is no weariness . . ."

There seemed to be no weariness in Rilke either. During
those days in Munich he looked young and refreshed and fitter
than ever. When I asked him if he had a quiet room and was able
to sleep, he said, "Oh, everything is right. There is still a vast
amount of sleep waiting for me. I have faith in it, almost as I
have in you; for through it my nature is still connected with
something deeply unspent and innocent."

At that time Rilke was still living a very retired life and

associated—apart from the Bruckmanns—with only one family, a mother and her two daughters, who lived some way out in Schwabing. He asked me once to go out there with him. I was attracted by the unusual atmosphere I found there and often repeated the visit. I was always received with great warmth and friendliness.

We never called the old lady anything but "the councillor's wife from Augsburg"[1]. Rilke said that, even if she bore no outward likeness to Goethe's mother, yet her cheerful, natural, unsophisticated manner resembled very closely to that of Frau Aja.

Always bright and active, this short, plump woman was popular with all the children in the Hofgarten. When she took her daily walk there after afternoon coffee, any child who crossed her path could be sure of getting a piece of chocolate or a sweet, which she produced from her capacious black velvet bag. In a smaller bag she carried bits of bread and scraps of all kinds to scatter to the dogs or the birds, whichever seemed in most need of them. Any visitor to her comfortable, old-fashioned flat was immediately regaled with delicious coffee, always followed by an invitation to dinner.

We would sit down at the round table to a simple meal and the "councillor's wife" would talk. Her fund of stories seemed inexhaustible—gay, exciting, grotesque and pathetic reminiscences of her own youth. One could listen to her for hours on end. Rilke would sit silent, leaning forward, watching her attentively.

"Her stories are always fresh and you never know how they will end," he once said in surprise. "The conclusion is always different from what you expected."

The two daughters did not in the least resemble their mother nor, indeed, each other. It was hard to believe that these three women were so closely related.

The younger daughter, a modest, friendly woman, had been a sister of mercy in the tropics and now lived with her mother and sister and acted as a private nurse. Rilke had told me that the elder sister was a remarkably gifted poet, and a stranger creature than this tall, angular young woman would be hard to imagine. Her clothes were of a rustic cut and as ageless as herself. Big,

[1] *Augsburger Frau Rat.*

black eyes enlivened her thin, almost peasant face, which often seemed frozen into an expression of profound melancholy. When a smile appeared on her wide, stern mouth, which happened rarely, she was even more heart-rending than when she stared in front of her, earnest and silent. Rilke told me that she wrote her verses and stories in a dream-state, half conscious, half somnambulistic. Although she could hardly be more than thirty, she had passed through an exceptionally severe, even horrible, experience that had nearly crushed her. Only a burning, almost fanatical piety, in which she believed she had found refuge from her misery, seemed to keep her going. Rilke did not know how far her ever cheerful and loving mother had been admitted to the girl's confidence, but the three women lived harmoniously and lovingly together, showing a mutual respect for each other despite the variety of their temperaments. Probably they kept many things concealed from each other but they were united in trust and tacit understanding.

Sometimes the poet read aloud to us in her hoarse and rather sing-song voice. Her verses often sounded to me as though she were speaking in her sleep—sometimes they seemed incoherent, yet they were full of deep wisdom. At her urgent request (as he said) Rilke had written a little foreword to her book. He had found the right words to introduce and elucidate what was a provisional, immature and yet somehow finished work. I admired the sympathy and power of penetration he brought to the task, and wrote down the main points of his introduction in my diary:

". . . You asked me to write an introduction to your book. I fulfill your wish because it is your wish and therefore I cannot believe that it can be quite unjustified, for no one can persuade me that you do not know what you want.

"An introduction, if I understand the word aright, has the object of preparing others, the readers, for what was your intention in this particular case. I can do only one thing: I can go before this intention and justify it. I cannot explain it. I can write: 'Whatever you encounter, accept it as true. Do not doubt (for I have never doubted)'.

"It is just this that determines, I think, the strange wonder that your work has induced in me, for in your writings even what is unexperienced, fallacious, unmastered, is endowed with a

certainty, so to speak with a purity of conscience, which admits of
no doubt. In such an accomplished period as ours one will seldom
find a poetic style composed of such contrary elements, for one
cannot admit that the finished stands side by side with the un-
finished; rather one would like to say that complete crudity is
inserted beneath sublime perfection, in such a way that what is
delightful, thus supported, comes into a stable and permanent
condition, into a sublime repose which one accepts without
question as eternal . . . If it were possible that anything so fine
could come from painting sheets of drawings, I should incline to
use for the moment this metaphor: that you spread a transparent
film of pure and permanent colour over figures and scenes drawn
with a strange clumsiness; that you do not keep everywhere to
the outlines of the drawings, which show a certain general and
superstitious conventionality, and in this way there is produced,
over the familiar and recognisable world, a world that is new and
unexpressed—your world.

"With this I have tried to justify—if you expected me to do so
—the publication of your poems, for if anyone is capable of
constructing his inner world as a whole, his achievement, cannot
as a reality among real things, be lastingly hidden. Now it is
obvious that this world, so early exposed, must be everywhere in
process of development. But just here perhaps I reach the centre
of my wonder, remembering that with you the provisional points
almost always to the final, as in a simile, and is its forerunner,
passionately filled with it.

"And yet the object is often so trifling that one is tempted to
regard it as mute and simple; but you cut a mouth in it and it
speaks greatly . . ."

I asked Rilke when he had written this, and he answered,
"In Paris, in 1908, in the middle of writing *Malte*."

So he had still found time to think of others and help them,
and the girl to whom he had offered this gift requited him with
her reverence and loyalty. That her works later disappeared, as
she herself did, was undoubtedly due to her unusual manner of
life, which could not stand up to reality. During my stay in
Munich she gave me Rilke's *Two Prague Stories*,[1] a very rare
book, nowhere obtainable, for it had long been out of print. I
knew how much she loved it and at first refused to accept such a

[1] '*Zwei Prager Geschichten*'.

gift. But she said, "It has been mine so long and has given me so much pleasure, it would be unfair if I still wanted to keep it for myself. Now you must take your pleasure in it."

And she wrote on the first page the following lines, which she had composed for me:

> "Friendship
> comes from afar . . .
> out of childhood . . .
> even there it
> shared our joys
> and then it went
> with us through the
> dark forests,
> confident,
> that it would find
> the great ocean
> at the end of them."[1]

Quite different and spacious in style was the hospitality of the Bruckmanns. Hugo Bruckmann, the well-known publisher, combined in his person the savant and the man of the world. The intellectual élite of Munich gathered round him and his clever wife, who before her marriage had been Princess Cantacuzène and was a real connoisseur of music and art. To their regular circle of friends belonged—apart from Rilke—Herr von Miller, president of the German Museum, and his family, Friedrich Klose and his wife, Courvoisier, Dr. Bodmer, the young and highly gifted Norbert von Hellingrat, Pigenot, Ludwig Klages and Alfred Schuler, who was the centre of violent conflicts. One often saw guests from a distance: Countess

---

[1] *Freundschaft*
kommt von weit her . . .
aus der Kindheit . . .
dort schon hat sie
unsere Freude geteilt
und dann ging sie
mit uns durch die
dunkeln Wälder,
vertrauensvoll,
dass sie das grosse Meer
an ihrem Ausgang
finden werde.

Blandine Gravina, daughter of Hans von Bülow, came from Bayreuth, and from Vienna the charming and brilliant Baron von Hess-Diller and his wife, a famous beauty and relative of the Bruckmanns, granddaughter of that Countess Giulietta Guicciardi to whom Beethoven dedicated his "Moonlight Sonata".

The magnificent rooms in the Bruckmanns' house at Carolinenplatz were built for large parties. In the spacious library groups would gather to discuss literature and questions of the day, while music was played in the great drawing-room. One moved freely and without constraint in an atmosphere of intellectual interests, which brought together artists and enthusiastic laymen.

Rilke did not often take part in the conversations and was sometimes merely a listener, yet his presence in itself determined the course of the conversation. It often seemed as though his spirit guided the talk without his intending it.

But when we were with our "councillor's wife" in Schwabing, he could discourse at length and come right out of himself in that small family circle.

Generally there were five of us. Sometimes Hans Carossa looked in for a while, after his consulting hours in the Theresienstrasse, and his arrival always brought with it something beautiful and a special sense of calm and steadiness. If we were worried about the fate of someone at the front and spoke of it to Carossa, we were ashamed of our fears. His confidence somehow lent one wings. I said to him once, "When you look at me, I dare not be afraid." His vision took in joy and pain with the same calm understanding. Once when I spoke of him, Rilke and I came to the same conclusion: the older he grew, the more Carossa in his inmost self would resemble that monk in the Indian legend.

Despite the war that time in Munich was a good and happy one. Unlike the previous occasion, our parting was full of confidence and was brightened by the coming joy of soon meeting again. For we intended to meet in Berlin, where I had to give a public concert and several concerts in hospitals. Meanwhile Rilke wrote me he would like to give some readings in Vienna, would I play on such an occasion? I agreed with the greatest readiness, but difficulties arose about the date and the hall, and finally, when almost everything was settled and arranged, Rilke said he could not make the journey.

I felt that something might have happened about which he did not wish to write. He had become restless, complained of sleeplessness and of "people, always more people", who disturbed and even harrassed him. ". . . just think, how deadly—I cannot be alone any more!" In my next letter I asked him why he did not guard his priceless solitude, as he had done in Paris. The answer was sad and alarming: "Ah, in Paris—there one lived in safe seclusion, no one came, but here! And the worst of it is that I cannot any longer say No!"

Months later, when I saw Rilke again in Berlin, I was shocked. He looked restless and tormented, and I soon found that he had become involved in a whirlpool of social engagements. It seemed suddenly to have become fashionable to invite "the famous Rilke". Especially the leading financiers outbid each other with invitations to tea, the theatre, luncheon. Rilke was asked his advice about the pictures they wished to buy; he had to hear the new star at the opera; a young dancer invited him to her first night; there was not an hour of the day when he was free to do as he pleased. During my first week in Berlin he came to us only once at Grunewald, and then he was harrassed and tired, and instead of resting, looked nervously at the clock before he had been with us an hour, for he had to be back by a certain time in Berlin.

"Ah, how much I should like to stay here today, but——"

"Rainer," I said, "take a rest for once. Say you will not go, if it is irksome." He looked at me uncertainly. "Would you say it for me? It would be splendid——" So I apologised by telephone to the butler of some Privy Councillor,[1] who would scarcely take my word for it, and wanted to send the car. Finally I managed to put him off and we spent a wonderful evening at home with Frau Delbrück and the children. Rilke was suddenly transformed; he became so light-hearted that he described to us how the Privy Councillor's car was perhaps standing at that moment outside the door of his house in the Marburger-strasse—and all in vain: ". . . it waits and waits, but I do not come, for I have vanished, like the man in Hans Andersen's fairy tale." The children wanted to know who that was, so Rilke told them the story of the flying trunk, of the journeys to far countries, and all at once we were in the wonderland of Egypt among pyramids and tombs of

---

[1] *Geheimrat.*

Kings. The children listened enthralled, with flushed cheeks, and when Rilke was speaking of the sun-cult of the young King Amenophis, he showed us two numbers of a periodical containing pictures of the latest excavations at Tel-el-Amarna. At last I saw the wonderful, almost flower-like features of that mysterious king, of whom Rilke had so often spoken and written to me. The boyish face had something infinitely moving, a mildness and loftiness without equal. It seemed as though he were himself a sun-god, radiating the light of his own being upon mankind. I was very glad when Rilke proposed that we should go in the next few days to the museum and see the bust of the king, which was there on loan; it was to be on exhibition for a short time only.

When Rilke had gone that evening, Berta Delbrück and I sat late in my room and I read her passages from a glorious letter he had written me about his visit to Egypt. It was the second letter I had received from him, written before we knew each other.

". . . look at the head of Amenophis IV in Berlin in the second glass court of the Egyptian Museum (I should have much to tell you about this king); feel through the medium of that face what it means to confront the infinite world and to develope in so restricted a space, through the intensified arrangement of a few details, an equilibrium with the whole universe. Could one not turn away from a starry night to find the same law flowering in this face, the same greatness, depth, unfathomableness? By looking at such things I learned to see, and when later, in Egypt, many of them stood before me in their extreme individuality, insight into them came to me in such waves that I lay almost the whole night long under the great Sphinx, as though before it I were cast out from my whole life. . . . I had no evening meal; the Arabs were sitting round their fire some way off and the darkness hid me from them. I had waited for nightfall out there in the desert; then I moved in slowly, the Sphinx at my back, reckoning that the moon must already be rising—for there was a full moon—behind the nearest pyramid, which was mightily illumined by the sunset glow. And when at last I had moved round it, not only was the moon already far up the sky, but it was pouring such a flood of light across the endless landscape that I had to shade my eyes with my hand in order to find my way between the heaps of rubble and excavations."

I looked up into Berta Delbrück's face and it seemed remote

N

and withdrawn. It was as though we were both listening to a voice, Rainer's voice. I went on:

". . . I looked for a place opposite that gigantic figure and lay there, wrapped in my cloak, alarmed, mysteriously participating. I do not know whether my existence ever came so fully into consciousness as in those nocturnal hours when it lost all its value. For what was it against all this? The dimension in which it moved had passed into obscurity; all that is world and existence was happening on a higher plane, where a god and a celestial body lingered silent, facing each other . . . here towered an image adjusted to the sky, on which thousands of years had no effect except a little contemptible decay, and the miracle was that this thing bore human features and in its sublime situation made shift with them. That countenance had assumed the habits of the cosmos; single parts of its look and smile were damaged, but the rising and setting of the skies had mirrored into it indestructible emotions.

"It took some time before my eyes conquered it, grasped its essence, achieved the mouth, the cheek, the forehead, on which moonlight and moonshade passed from expression to expression . . . but there, as I gazed at it again, in some unexpected way I was taken into its confidence; then I began to know that cheek, then I experienced it in the perfect feeling of its curve . . . think of this: Behind the projection of the royal hood on the head of the Sphinx, an owl had flown up and had slowly, indescribably audibly in the clear depth of the night, touched the face in its soft flight; and now the contour of that cheek was laid on my hearing, which in the hours of night-stillness had grown very acute, as though etched on it by a miracle . . ."

A few days later Rilke and I were really standing in the glass-court of the Egyptian Museum, and there in the middle, softly lighted from all sides and from above, the head of the king rose up from a simple pedestal. The bust is a perfectly preserved sculptor's model in fine limestone: a face of indescribable beauty. The eyes, modelled sightless, seem yet to look at the observer with an expression of the deepest wisdom and dreamlike goodness, a goodness that radiates through the whole boyish face. One realises that this founder of a new religion was devoted to the cult of the sun and believed in the omnipotent radiation of that great, life-sustaining body.

Now I understood Rilke's words: "Could one not turn away from a starry night and find the same law flowering in this face?"

Other magnificent finds were on view at the exhibition; the portrait of the Queen-Mother Teye and a relief depicting the king himself with his family, the sun shining upon them and its beams ending in little blessing hands. But I had to return again and again to the bust and contemplate that tranquil, sublime face.

Shortly after our visit to the museum I held my concert before a large audience in the Klindworth-Scharwenka Hall. My dear Titi Taxis was there and Marie Bülow—Hans von Bülow's widow. I also saw the Delbrücks, Albrecht Schaeffer, Ossip Schubin, my Nostiz friends from Leipzig, our ambassador, Prince Hohenlohe, and his wife, and many other familiar faces. All had made contributions for the wounded, and from money collected at the concert I was able to give several soldiers a four-weeks' stay at a health resort to complete their convalescence.

It was a fine, serious occasion and the impression the music made on the audience gave me great pleasure. I knew why: Rainer sat exactly opposite me on the seat next to the centre aisle. After the first notes I forgot the hall and the people and the concert; I was conscious only of us three—the music and Rilke and myself. The deep emotion he felt at the music streamed across to me so that I played *him*, and him only!

The others may have sensed this unconsciously or by some intuition and felt that it was not only the minds of Bach and Mozart and Liszt that raised them all to a state of joy or sadness, according to their individual temperaments, but also the soul of Rilke.

After the concert we spent some time with a few friends before Rilke took me home by car. As we were nearing the Grunewald house, he said, "Did you really play only for me? May I believe that as firmly as I felt it the whole evening?"

He had known it all, and I answered, "I have always played for you since I have known you, for you are bound up inseparably with all the pain and happiness of music." Rilke accompanied me through the dark outer garden to the house and waited till I had unlocked the door. We took each other's hands and he said almost inaudibly and very earnestly, "Your music—I can never thank you enough for it. Perhaps another, a very great man and a far one, will tell you before the day is out what I cannot express because it is too deep for me." Then he closed the garden door.

I went softly through the hall and into my room, trying to avoid waking anyone, completely filled with the enigmatic words Rilke had spoken at parting. Upstairs I put on the light and as the lamp shone out I suddenly understood with deep, startled joy and emotion what he had meant—in front of me on the table was Amenophis, a most wonderful reproduction of the kingly bust from the Egyptian Museum, overhung by the tall stem of a rose with open petals coloured like the dawn!

When I found Rilke's gift in my room that night I did not dream that I had spent with him the last beautiful and harmonious day we were ever to have together. Occupied with professional affairs, we saw each other only once more before I left Berlin, and that was at a big reception among a crowd of strangers and acquaintances to whom we were indifferent. Rilke was profoundly changed; he seemed shy and irritable. When we had an uninterrupted moment together and could exchange a word or two alone, I begged him urgently to free himself from the many irksome social duties that were harassing him.

"Yes, if only *you* could always refuse them with the warm resolution you showed the other evening, I should be almost saved," he said. But I saw none the less that he was again seeking intercourse with other people, though he had complained a few days before: "Oh, they show me around at dinner as though I were a Sèvres vase or a silver epergne that someone has rummaged out and thinks valuable."

"People have taken possession of me and will not let me go," he wrote me later, and said he would escape to Munich again and stay there for good, ". . . secluded, alone—ah, to be able to be alone, I scarcely know any longer what it means!"

He had come out of his solitude and found himself among people, and they avenged themselves for all the years he had withheld himself from them.

Rilke had changed still more when I saw him again in Munich a year later. He was really scarcely ever alone, always accompanied by someone who made claims upon him, who wanted to be saved or comforted. He told me of a woman, a painter, whom he often saw and who wanted his help. "Do you know?" he said repeatedly. "It makes me so weary and is such a responsibility, but what am I to do?"

He never spoke again of his work. If his protégés gave him a little peace, he went to art-galleries or stood in the *Pinakothek*, looking at the paintings of Greco and Breughel, deep in troubled thought. Once we met by chance at an exhibition; I did not want to intrude on him and tried to leave unnoticed, but he caught sight of me and came up. "Look at that strange work by Munch," he said, and pointed to an etching on the wall in front of us: many hands raised in supplication or challenge, all straining upward, beside and above each other, as though striving to reach the same goal, till, right at the top, only two hands remained, outstretched in a gesture of despair—and above them was a coffin. "Ghastly!" I cried. Rilke smiled sadly. "That picture is entitled 'Fame'," he answered. "It is terribly true, for what remains?—A coffin!"

Nevertheless, even in those days I succeeded in cheering him. One of my young friends had written a cycle of poems that seemed to me beautiful and significant. When I read them to him Rilke fully agreed and I resolved to have them printed privately as a small collectors' object, and to send a copy in a specially fine binding to my young friend as a surprise Christmas present.

We spent several mornings at printers' and bookbinders', selecting types and looking at bindings. Rilke suggested that purple kid would be very attractive and suitable. He had once been presented with one of his own books in a fine binding of this kind. A few days later a messenger brought me a short letter from Rainer with a bunch of white cyclamen:

"In Munich, or (in other words), somewhere in Tunis!

" 'Sixty to eighty marks', Herr Stobbe has just told me on the telephone. So the whole thing (if you add a medium-sized purple kid or other better-class binding-beast) ought really to be obtainable for about a hundred marks.

"But what news from Lehmkuhl?

"Looking forward with great discretion to Your Grace's further orders,

"one-bashfully-bound-in-the-finest-oasis-kid."

This sweet, light-hearted state of mind soon changed again. He grew tired and irritable and complained again and again that the woman-painter, who had followed him to Munich, constantly plagued him with her restlessness. She wanted to paint him; she wanted to persuade him to travel with her—he did not know what to do. Would I care to see her and let him know what sort of impression she made on *me*? She was a pitiful creature, had a partially crippled foot and was often ill.

Those were miserable days. Suddenly, before any solution could be found, I had to leave for Hamburg to play a piano concerto of Beethoven's. The conductor was on the point of being conscripted for the army, and the concert had to take place earlier than had been planned.

We said good-bye in the foyer of the Prinz-regenten Theater in Munich on the evening before I left, unaware that it was to be good-bye for ever. I had two seats for *Parsifal*. At first Rilke wanted to come with me, but at the last moment he could not bring himself to listen to it; he suddenly feared that he would be "overwhelmed and seduced" by Wagner's music, and would spend a sleepless night. He asked whether I should be passing through Munich on the way back from Hamburg. "Yes, in eight days I shall be here again for a little while, so fare you well, Rainer."

"Come soon, Benvenuta—as soon as you can."

He had never tried to persuade anyone to do anything. It was the first time he had made so urgent a request. At the door he turned again and waved to me. That was our parting.

My plan to travel home via Munich came to nought. Unexpectedly I had to play in Königsberg, and from there I went direct to Budapest, to the funeral of a near relative who had suddenly died. When, after a depressing time, I got home again, I found a letter from Rilke with the *Book of Hours*, of which I had so often bought copies and given them away and now no longer possessed one.

The copy Rilke sent me was in a costly binding of red tanned leather with narrow vertical stripes of black and gold. My name was blocked on the spine in little gold letters.

"So, instead of me, here is the much delayed *Book of Hours*—yours. In a stout dress and with words that will prevent your giving it away. Thus, a permanent possession," he wrote. The lines in the *Book of Hours*, written with his own hand, were these:

"If, as of old, we won it on our knees,
   long from God's spirit I drew sustenance,
   but now the *marching* lords dispense decrees
   and on our feet we owe obedience.

"Lagging behind the rest I thus am driven,
   I never learned upon my knees to climb.
   But just as once the kneeling were forgiven
   so now are walkers guiltless of their time."[1]

Conditions grew more and more serious and tragic. I was
working with a number of pupils, trying to find strength and
solace in our art. We dared not think of the future.

Rilke still wrote now and then, but presently his letters ceased.
Common friends told me he had been called up to the army and
had fainted in the course of some strenuous exercise. He was
now engaged in clerical duties. The news moved me deeply.
How could he stand such tests with his uncertain health? How
intense must be his mental suffering!

About that time I had one more glimpse of Rilke. It was in
Vienna, about midday, in a busy street of the inner town.

He came towards me without seeing me. A woman was
clinging to his arm, a woman with a faded, ageing face daubed
with make-up. She was limping and leaning heavily on his arm.
Then he saw me: the bright eyes in his deadened face lit up
suddenly with alarm and he looked at me with an expression of
torment and unutterable dismay. The woman at his side must
have seen it, for she said something and her mouth curled with
mockery. He lowered his head, then other people thrust themselves between us and they were both lost to sight. But it seemed
to me that something beautiful had suddenly died, something I
still carried in my heart despite all the distances that had
separated us. Rainer had passed me by without a word.

---

[1] *Erränge man's wie einst als Hingeknieter,*
ich lebte längst aus Gottes Geist,
doch jetzt befiehlt ein schreitender Gebieter
der uns im Gehn gehorchen heisst.

Da ebbli ich weit hinter den anderen,
denn ich kann nicht gehn auf meinen Knien.
Aber wie einst den kniend Schreitenden
ist jetzt den Gehenden die Zeit verziehn.

In the years that followed life became progressively harder. The war seemed incapable of ending, the misery grew ever greater. Young, radiant Norbert Hellingrat had fallen; Walter Heymel was dead; my youngest and dearest cousin was missing. Carl had come home seriously wounded, but there was some hope of complete recovery, and Maria, glad to have him back, nursed him with selfless devotion.

I heard from my friend Elizabeth that Rilke had been released from military service and had gone to Switzerland, where he was taking up his work again. I did not believe it, I felt as though he were infinitely far away, on another planet. All the same I was still able to do something for him that might bring him a little pleasure and relief, though he did not know who was responsible for it. I wrote to my relatives in Switzerland, telling them that Rilke had had to leave all his belongings in Paris at the outbreak of war, and that I had learned that the books and furniture in his flat had been publicly auctioned. This letter caused Romain Rolland, who was a close friend of my uncle, to go secretly to Paris—it was said that in France there was a price on his head on account of his convictions—with the object of looking after Rilke's affairs. Some time later my uncle informed me that Rolland had succeeded, after innumerable visits to second-hand furniture-dealers in Paris, in buying back some of Rilke's belongings.

Duse's letters and many other valuable papers had gone unrecognised and had apparently been destroyed. They were never found.

Amidst all the suffering of that time so many things had lost their value that one hardly dared worry about such things. The war was over and one had to do one's best to cope with the problems of the day.

Epilogue

IN 1926 I was invited to spend Christmas at an estate in the country. My friend and her housekeeper lived alone in a big mansion that had once been built for a family with many children and grandchildren. Now the two upper floors, which were very comfortably furnished, served as guest-rooms. A music-room, a conservatory, a terrace-room and a dining-room, with living-rooms and bedrooms, were in that part of the house occupied by the two ladies. A spacious library completed the suite, and at the end of the corridor was the Goethe Room, the finest in the whole house. Silhouettes, first editions of the works of Goethe and Schiller, furniture from Goethe's Weimar period, pictures, candles with painted shades, carried me back into an earlier century. The great windows were lightly hung with white muslin curtains and afforded a view across the garden, which lost itself in the depths of an expanse of woodland and reminded one, with its little swan-lakes and pavilions, of the park at Tiefurt.

Now in winter the Bohemian uplands were covered with snow; the ponds were frozen and huge beech-logs from the woods of the estate burned day and night in the big tiled stove. When we had driven by sledge along the lonely forest roads to the nearest town, we came home refreshed, to enjoy the warmth and comfort of a house that breathed of kindness and true humanity. My friend and I often sat by the fire in the Goethe Room after the rest of the party had gone to bed. She made dolls' clothes for the occupants of a children's home; the big St. Bernard was with the gardener on his final rounds of the park and stables and, until "Rolf" came back and the house was locked up, we talked or I read aloud to her. She loved Goethe and Shakespeare more than any others, and especially she wanted to hear me read Goethe's *Correspondence with a Child*.[1] I had with me the copy given me by Rilke in Paris, and, as I read, my thoughts often went out to him, the hermit of Muzot, who once would have enjoyed these

[1] *Briefwechsel mit einem Kinde.*

tranquil hours and derived from them such pleasure and gratitude. Was he still in a position to do so?

It was years since I had heard from him. But I had learned from others that he was now living in a country house near Sierre in the Valais valley, and had finished the elegies. Once a little parcel, addressed in an unfamiliar hand, reached me from Switzerland. It contained the elegies and the sonnets to Orpheus, but no letter or sign of any kind.

On Christmas Eve Carl wrote me that Maria and he were with the children at Montreux. He had heard that Rilke was there too, in a sanatorium. Carl had not seen him, but people had reported with great concern that Rilke was very ill. Did I know of his condition? And did I sometimes hear from him?—No, I did not.

Then came the sweet feast of Christmas and all its hundred activities absorbed my thoughts. First we had to distribute the presents at the children's home and listen to their little songs and recitations. I was touched by the happy faces of the children as they received shyly and happily the gifts chosen with so much love. Beautiful was the walk through the dark garden to the old town wall, where the remains of Wallenstein's castle adjoined the church. One could go straight through a little doorway in the park-wall to the organ-loft. It had snowed all day, then the moon broke through wind-tattered cloud. Fresh snow cloaked hedges, door-posts, branches and corners of walls; the meadows lay shining white under a starry sky. The little Gothic church was brightly lit with wax candles, which cast a warm glow on the ornaments of the golden altar and the wreaths of fir. There was an odour of incense and Christmas trees. I took my seat at the organ and, before matins began, the venerable psalm "We praise Thee, O Lord", sung by voices high and deep, rolled over the assembled people, and to my inner eye a distant and unknown house appeared, a simple room, a bed where a sick man moaned perhaps in fever. And I played for him, as though after all those years and across the intervening space he could hear me again, playing a hymn of comfort and light.

When we came out of the church the moon had vanished. We lit our lanterns and walked through the crunching snow while fresh flakes floated noiselessly from the sky. We went down the steps by the gate in the wall, entered the park and reached the warm house, full of the smells of Christmas cakes, apples and fir branches.

There were many guests during Christmas, and shortly before New Year's Eve—which my friend always spent alone, as the old custom required, arranging her letters and her memories and taking stock of the past year—all her friends and the chief people of the little town came to dinner again. We sang, read and made music, and it was not till long after midnight that we accompanied the guests to the courtyard, where carriages and sledges were waiting to take them to their homes.

Despite the late hour I had no wish to go to bed, so I arranged various things in my room and read the magnificent dialogue between Vittoria Colonna and Michelangelo in Gobineau's *Renaissance*. More than an hour must have passed thus before I put out the light.

Soon after falling asleep, I was awakened by a loud cry: it was as though someone outside had called my name in deadly fear. I rushed to the window and threw open both casements. The garden was still as death, lawns and trees shimmering pale in the darkness under their load of snow; from the church beyond, five strokes sounded through the clear, icy air. So it would soon be morning. Shivering with cold, I shut the window and lay down again. Hardly knowing what I was doing, half drunk with sleep, I folded my hands and prayed, "Whoever you are who called me, I bless you and I am near you. God help you in your need!"

Then the warm safety of the room enfolded me and I fell asleep again.

But in that hour Rainer Maria Rilke died. . . .

Months later I received by the hand of a stranger the letters I had written him. I sorted them and was on the point of locking them up in a little press, when I caught sight of a narrow blue envelope on which was written in Rilke's hand: *dernière lettre à B.*

Our encounter in Vienna had intruded between us like an invisible wall, and in all the years of silent separation no word had passed between us. Now, suddenly, I held in my hand a letter from him, like a message from another world. A last message of whose contents I had no knowledge. Was it a greeting, a friendly thought—or a reproach?

Many days passed before I dared open the letter—and then with the knowledge of his love, concealed for years, unexhausted and inexhaustible, the pain broke through and flooded my heart with undreamed-of power:

". . . once you wrote me of a little song that made you cry as a child. Do you remember, Benvenuta? It ran:

> " 'I tried to find you everywhere
> by wood and field and tide—
> I found you not, for you must be
> too deep my heart inside'.[1]

" 'I tried to find you everywhere' . . . You see, there I stood, stood and mistrusted my soul and mistrusted my body and mistrusted my vain searching—and could not write, for there was always my all-too-heavy heart towards you, my heart, perhaps long since condemned and dying—only my heart—no words— not *one* word—and my heart I could not write. Much has become buried and can hardly be told, but if, one day, the hour you know of should come (and it is certain that I could then do no other than unquestioningly affirm it), then bear testimony, for you are called to be my witness, you who hold the legacy of my life in your blessed hands.

"And I—under the influence of your radiant being all that is twisted, all that is irreparably and inexorably injured in my nature has become for ever clear. There you were, Benvenuta, my star, and wanted to shine for me on my battle, my victory. But I was not like Joshua and did not *dare* and did not trust my power to *stop the sun*.

"But if I never achieved that, at least God has led me to the mountain-top and shown me you. *You, Benvenuta!* And who could ever again take from me what I have seen? Even death can only lock it up inside me . . ."

(Letter to the dead.)   August, 1928.
Rainer! I have come to you in order to be near you again, not near in heart, no long journey would be required for that, for

---

[1] *Ich hab Dich überall gesucht*
in Wald und Flur und Hain—
ich fand Dich nicht, Du musst mir wohl
zu tief im Herzen sein.

where could you be more present and more real than in the loving
gratefulness of my memory? No, I have come to you to see the
house where you lived and the little churchyard, afar from the
world, where you are buried. It has been a long journey, over
uplands and through valleys, past towns and villages and landscapes. Some of them we once saw together on our journey
from Paris to Venice. It is strangely sad and full of mystery to
think that we travelled together past that high-built village of
Raron, where years later you were to find rest from the hardships
of your life. We may even have seen the gold cross on its spire,
sparkling in the sunshine, but without intimation that your
destiny would find its end at that church and on that lonely
height. We may have seen too the little castle in the peaceful
valley of Sierre, where you were to finish the work of your greatest
yearning and agony, the elegies.

When, on my way to you, I left the train at Sierre station and
inquired for the castle of Muzot, a child directed me to it as though
you were still alive, and I took the rustic path towards the hill,
through the wide hill country and the brilliant morning, between
pastures and by big clumps of trees. There was no one in sight;
in the village the bells were calling to worship and the house-
doors were shut. Only one young woman came towards me; she
seemed to have been delayed and was on her way to church. She
wore her Sunday best, a black silk dress and a black kerchief, and
walked with free and gracious bearing unhurriedly towards the
valley. As we met, she looked me in the face, and said with an
indescribably gentle gravity, *"Bon jour, ma sœur!"* It was as
though the spirit of your rich sympathy had touched her, inspiring
her to this simple greeting. I was moved and thanked her; it
seemed for a moment that she would take my hand, then she
walked on.

When I caught sight of Muzot, as it gazed from its height across
the wide valley, like a watch-tower, I had to stop and take that
prospect whole into my heart. That lonely and ancient guardian,
standing in heroic surroundings, had watched over and protected
the last struggling years of your life, and it seemed still to protect
the memory of your peace and seclusion, for when I got there
and went through the garden gate, I found the door locked.

"Monsieur Rilke's housekeeper has gone to church," said a
peasant who was passing with his dog—and he too spoke of you

as though you were still living. Yes, you were everywhere: the beautiful, shady vine-bower spoke of you, and the carefully tended, tall-stemmed roses of your garden smelt as though they bloomed for you. Even the little spring remembered how often you had listened to the plash of its water making the quietude around you still quieter.

So I sat in your garden, a long time, till the sun climbed to noon. No other person went by, and the woman did not come back. But although I could not see your house and your room, I was thankful to be alone and knew, when I went, that those hours in your garden had become my own, my very own, and I could never lose them.

And next day I took the final step to you: I went to the church at Raron and made my pilgrimage to your grave.

I stood in the lonely churchyard, high above the valley, surrounded by the mightiest works of nature, and it looks as if it had been blown on to their crags. I looked for your resting-place there and did not find it among the few poor graves. There were no flowers on them, either because they were neglected or because the wind that blows here so often will tolerate no peaceful blossoming. I was on my way to the church-door, looking for someone who could point out your grave, when I saw a little mound beside the wall of the tower, in a spot better protected from the storms and overgrown with purple petunias. The poor little cross of rough wood bore no inscription except the almost illegible letters, engraved by a clumsy, peasant hand: R.M.R.

Dear, dear Rainer, that little cross above your grave moved me more deeply than all the sad and cruel things that have befallen me in all my life. But even then a word of yours cured my pain and stopped my tears, shining in my heart like a message from your world: ". . . for poverty is a great brightness from within . . ."

Here you rested, who have known, more deeply than most men, pilgrimage, poverty and death. Perhaps it is the ultimate meaning of your life and of your immortality that you are bedded far from the world, in a serene stillness, where only the storms speak and the moonlight broods, bedded there like the coolness of radiant mornings, or the shimmering air of summer noontides, or the soft mutations of the sky from sunshine to starlight.

I touched with my hands the earth under which you sleep and

I spoke to you. I told you that through you my life has gained inner wealth and blessings beyond compare, for you have taught me to see and understand. You have taught me the meaning of greatness and suffering and happiness and renunciation. You have taught me what kindness and hardness are. All the gates of life you have opened to me, and only thus could I enter into my own life, that has found fulfilment and certainty. It is true that it was not till I was far away from you that I found the way to that undivided world, to that high heart, for which I once prayed in a time of despair, and which fate gave me years later, as though by a miracle. All this I said to you beside your grave—and I felt that now you would forgive me the last breath of melancholy that might still remain between us somewhere in the unfathomed depths of being; that you knew why nothing but the superhuman could be constant and permanent between us.

The superhuman has its own measure and is exposed to all the misunderstandings of the world, yet deep down it is secure in the unwritten laws of eternity and only there has it validity and fulfilment.

My last word to you is like my first, written in that first letter I sent out to you in the unknown distance; and now it goes a greater distance to you, beyond the stars than we mortals can reckon. It is a word I shall keep alive in my heart as long as I breathe:

Thanks!

Benvenuta.